4000s by 40

4000s by 40

Tackling Middle Age in the Mountains of New Hampshire

Matt Larson

Copyright © 2024 by Matt Larson
All rights reserved, including the right of reproduction in whole or in part in any form. For information about permission to reproduce selections from this book, write to Vandreren Publishing LLC at: 360 Route 101, Bldg 1, Bedford, NH 03110

ISBN: 978-1-7346774-0-9

For Chloe, Max, Jake, and Phoebe

Many climbs lie ahead of you. Give yourself fully to each of them, enjoy them, and befriend the people you meet along the way; you will always have stories to tell and friends to share them with.

"Live your life so that the fear of death can never enter your heart."
—Chief Tecumseh

The "48" 4000-footers of New Hampshire

Washington – 6288'
Adams – 5774'
Jefferson – 5712'
Monroe – 5384'
Madison – 5367'
Lafayette – 5260'
Lincoln – 5089'
South Twin – 4902'
Carter Dome – 4832'
Moosilauke – 4802'
Eisenhower – 4780'
North Twin – 4761'
Carrigain – 4700'
Bond – 4698'
Middle Carter – 4610'
West Bond – 4540'
Garfield – 4500'
Liberty – 4459'
South Carter – 4430'
Wildcat – 4422'
Hancock – 4420'
South Kinsman – 4358'
Osceola – 4340'
Field – 4340'

Flume – 4328'
South Hancock – 4319'
Pierce – 4310'
North Kinsman – 4293'
Willey – 4285'
Bondcliff – 4265'
Zealand – 4260'
North Tripyramid – 4180'
Cabot – 4170'
East Osceola – 4156'
Middle Tripyramid – 4140'
Cannon – 4100'
Hale – 4054'
Jackson – 4052'
Tom – 4051'
Wildcat D – 4050'
Moriah – 4049'
Passaconaway – 4043'
Owl's Head – 4025'
Galehead – 4024'
Whiteface – 4020'
Waumbek – 4006'
Isolation – 4004'
Tecumseh – 4003'

*Surveyed heights of the 4000-footers continue to change. The heights recorded here were compiled from the understood heights at the time each mountain was climbed.

Author's Note

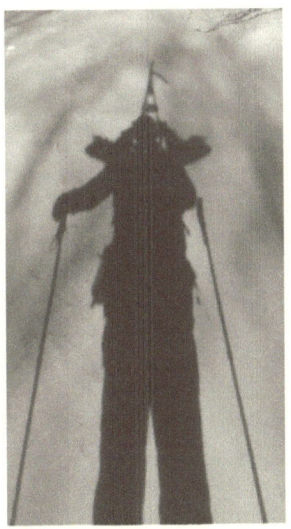

Life interrupted this book more than once, changing its course a few times along the way. To keep it all straight, I drew from direct memory, my journals, the audio memos I recorded during my climbs, and conversations with some of the people mentioned. Some names in the pages that follow have been altered to protect their privacy. The contents of this book express the opinions and recollections of the author alone.

Prologue

The Wandering Idiot

Let me state for the record that I am no Cheryl Strayed. I've never used heroin, never had an affair, and barring an exceptional case of Napoleon complex when I was twelve, have more or less pretty much always had my shit together. Sure, I've had my bumps here and there, but no major life adversity sent me running for the hills: I didn't grow up on food stamps, didn't get left for dead in the jungles of Colombia, and I didn't get thrown in jail for a crime I didn't commit. In my naïve youth I sometimes wished that I had some major conflict like that to fight against. To state my cause against. Of course, now I know better. Yet despite this knowledge, and roughly thirty-eight years of grounded living—*by society's standards*—there I was, alone at forty-six hundred feet in below-freezing temperatures, still climbing upwards.

Emerging above the treeline, windswept snow canvassed the open space before me like ocean waves that never got the chance to break. It felt like I was standing on the moon. My pack became weightless, and I took this moment to appreciate myself for being such a badass. *Woohoo! Nobody up here but me!* But then I looked northward at the darkening sky—I was stunned. Thick layers of clouds were sweeping up and over the mountain, completely obscuring what I now discerned to be the true summit. Suddenly I felt very tired; fatigue sets in fairly quickly when you arrive at what you thought was the finish line and learn you have quite a ways to go.

This was a good moment to pause and assess the situation. Dropping my pack to the ground, I opened it in search of hydration and ideas. *Maybe it's not as far as it looks*, I thought. *Maybe the storm is about to peel off.* As I stood there trying to quell self-doubt, a blast of wind picked up the snowpack around me and slapped me in the face with a million tiny ice bullets. Clearing the shrapnel from my eyes, I could see it was now snowing at the summit. *Oh, great.* Then I discovered my Gatorade reserves had frozen during the last hour of climbing, and any remaining optimism fizzled out of me.

With some vigorous finger tapping and a few whaps against my hiking boot, it finally relinquished some drops of nourishment, but the revelation of the petrified Gatorade was far more sobering than the imminent snowstorm. Only one other bottle of water remained inside my pack, and it too was a complete brick of ice. *How did I not think of this?* A part of me, well, most of me, would have kept going if my supplies were ample and still liquid, but I immediately started to question if I could make summit without any fluids. Strike one.

Pulling out my cellphone to update Mission Control (aka my wife Liz at home with our four kids), I noticed the battery life was at 2%. *Fricking HTC piece of crap!* Should something go wrong, and I get stranded up here with no way to call for help, Mission Control would not be pleased. This was also the first big solo climb that was wife-approved, and if I went radio silent, I didn't know how long I had before helicopters and search teams would start canvassing the area for me. I did *NOT* want to show up as a missing hiker on New Hampshire's 6pm news, even if I was missing. Strike two.

Further amplifying my concern was the fact that there was nobody around for miles. I'd only seen one person all day: a snowshoe runner named Alex? Alec? Andy? We could hardly contain ourselves when we came across each other, as if we were the only two guys to discover the secret to life's greatest mysteries.

"Hey!" he yelled out. "How you doin'?"

"Great," I replied, "this is unbelievable, isn't it?"

"Yeah! I just got these snowshoes for Christmas and this is my first chance to try them out. This is awesome!"

"It sure is, man!" For some reason I always say "man" on the trail as if I'm sixteen again. "No worries" slips out a lot as well. But my run-in with Alex was over two hours ago and he was long gone. If something did happen to me, it would be at least a day, if not longer, before anybody came by. The worries were beginning to pile up. Strike three.

Decision time. I jogged up past the last hook of spruces to get a better look at the remaining distance, but the closer view offered no encouragement. With all of the cloud cover, I didn't have a clue how long it would take to summit. Maybe an hour? Maybe two? At either rate, not enough time to make it up and back down again before nightfall. Strike four. A hitter can still make it to first base on a dropped strike three, but you never get a chance to see a strike four. Texting Mission Control that I was heading back down, I watched with dread as my phone went black the moment I hit send. *Uh oh, I'm in trouble.* It was time to go.

Strapped to my pack was a pair of Blizzard skis with bright orange Technica ski boots clipped into the bindings for even weight distribution. The bottoms of the Blizzards were set into the outside pockets, normally reserved for carrying drinks, while the tips were lashed together with a strip of Velcro-actioned rope I had acquired from The Home Depot. The arrangement formed what looked like a giant letter "A" on my pack, which I thought looked pretty dang cool. What wasn't cool was finding out that the linings of each ski boot were as frozen as my Gatorade. No amount of ramming or twisting could get my feet in past the ankle sections of either boot. Strike five.

Damn it! Only an hour earlier I had been in a state of euphoria, my steps buoyed by the sun dappling through the trees. Endorphins crescendoing, I found myself bellowing out the lyrics to Bill Withers' "Use me." After that soaring rendition, and feeling quite comfortably alone in the woods, I stuck with Bill Withers for my next performance and sang "Lean on Me" at the top of my lungs. For an encore I made some off-key attempts at Stevie Wonder's "Signed, Sealed, Delivered, I'm Yours," muddling all the lyrics while maintaining peak volume. I didn't have a choice in the matter: it was a soul music kinda day.

Now the music was gone. I cursed my boots and my stupidity. I was embarrassed. Not a single soul around and I was embarrassed. To whom? To all the backcountry skiers who would have questioned me carrying my skis instead of skinning up? To the rescuers collecting my corpse? To Liz, who I would tell the whole ordeal to, even though I didn't have to? To Fridtjof Nansen, my Norwegian hero? To God? To my other self?

My only option to get off the mountain before dark was to ski, so I frantically started working the boot linings back and forth. Weather reports that day said the temperature would range between thirteen and twenty degrees at the base of the mountain, and my guess was that it was approaching zero where I was. After all that effort to get up there, the idea of having to carry my skis back down in the bitter dark was unacceptable. Besides, skiing down was the whole point!

Since I didn't make summit, I had no choice but to return the way I came. The trail I was *supposed* to ski down, the Carriage Road, was reportedly wide and ideal for backcountry turns. The Gorge Brook? Not so much. It zigzagged back and forth the whole way, a parkour course of hairpin turns and exposed rocks. In my Google research, I had not read of a single soul skiing down it, yet here I was, my back stiffening with the dropping temperatures, my ankle bleeding from a ski boot that wouldn't give, preparing to do something I had absolutely no preparation for. It was in this moment, looking forlornly at my rigid boots, that I concluded I was, in fact, an idiot.

Seconds felt like minutes as my mind drew a blank. *How are we going to get ourselves out of this one, Matt?* The half-frozen sandwich I ate an hour earlier turned over in my stomach, and the taste of nickels hit the back of my throat. I swallowed and went to work. After twenty minutes of wagging the boot tongues, I managed to rake my ankles through, cutting my shins in several places upon entry. It reminded me of ski boots from the eighties. Despite being physically wrung out and in pain, I felt incredible relief knowing my feet were finally in there. Now came the hard part.

The previous winter I replaced my very old, very long K2s with a pair of Blizzard "Bushwackers." Snapping my boots into the bindings, I was supremely grateful for the change. The Blizzards were significantly lighter and shorter, and within minutes of my descent, it was clear that I couldn't have done it with the K2s. As it was, I fell three times because there was hardly any room to turn. Worse still, the trail, which had good hard-packed snow and was soft on the feet hiking up, had completely iced over with the disappearing sun and the late afternoon chill. It was a luge. The only way to manage it was to snowplow at a hellacious speed before quickly shifting to french fries at each turn. Around one tight bend I caught my tips on a thin birch and went careening down on my keester, coming inches away from knocking my head on a massive boulder. That's when I realized I should have brought a helmet. Strike six.

I reached the base of the mountain in roughly forty minutes, my skis suffering some nice gouges along the way. My back ached from the awkward turns and my body was spent. Unfortunately, I still had to hike another two miles down the entry road, which I never anticipated being closed off to cars for the winter. With snow on the ground and skis on my back, it was an energy expense I could have done without. Strike seven. Well before I got back to the truck, I decided that if I was going to be a real outdoorsman, I was going to have to get a lot better at googling these climbs beforehand.

A few days later, probably because my body was so worn down from the first real bit of exercise I had done in a year, I got my first case of strep throat. Living with four kids was likely the real culprit, but I love them, so I'll blame Moosilauke. It turned out to be a bad case too and I couldn't kick it for over a month. By the time I recovered, I was fully immersed again in family and work, focusing my time and energy on coaching tee-ball and paying the bills. Thoughts of climbing leapt from the front of my mind and hopped into the back seat of my brain . . . an itch to scratch another day.

Chapter 1

A Plan Awakens

Over dinner one night at the Texas Roadhouse in Nashua, two weeks before my misadventures on Moosilauke, I announced to my wife, children, and parents that I wanted to climb all forty-eight of the 4000-foot mountains in New Hampshire before I turned forty years old. It was a month before my thirty-eighth birthday.

"I think that's great, Matt. Maybe I will do some with you," said my mom, who to my knowledge at age sixty-five, had never climbed a single mountain in her life. My kids and my dad just stared at me for a moment and then went back to eating their mac n' cheese dinners. Yes, all of them.

The only reaction that really mattered to me though was my wife Liz's, which turned out to be extremely supportive but surprised. "I had no idea," she said. "Okay, go for it." *Wait, what? Did I hear that correctly? No idea?* I was positive that I had expressed my desire to climb the 4000-footers before. Ever since I was a kid, I wanted to climb them, and even climbed a couple of them with Liz when we first started dating. Surely, I mentioned something about it then?

Before we had kids, Liz and I used to go hiking for ten hours at a time, sometimes more. We climbed Lafayette and Lincoln. We tackled a seventeen-hour day in Paintbrush Canyon in Wyoming. We even climbed Mt. Rainier together, which to this day is still the hardest single ascent I've ever done. Through all of these hikes and more, we trudged up and down mountain ridges, contemplated life, made goals, and endured monotonous marches where I was bound to repeat some life philosophy that I had rattled on about already. My desire to climb the 4000-footers of New Hampshire had to have come up before. *No idea?!* I resolved to work on my communication skills.

An outdoor enthusiast herself, Liz has always been very athletic, though she'll discount me saying so and tell you otherwise. Don't believe her. In the previous decade she ran four marathons and coached me through my one marathon, so she appreciates the concept of tackling something both mentally and physically challenging, to say the least. She would have been very happy to climb the 4000-footers as well, but she knew I had some strange need to get out there and test myself, and unfortunately with the kids being as young as they were, it wasn't likely we'd get much time to climb together anytime soon. Plus, her knee hadn't been cooperating lately.

When I declared my plan, Liz's positivity was what I was hoping for and half-expected, but I was relieved to hear her say it out loud. If I was going to do this she needed to be on board, because the time involved can infringe upon happiness in the home. I think what surprised her was not my desire to climb the 4000-footers, but to do it so soon. She didn't know it at the time, but I, like every man before me, was already squirming at the idea of turning forty. I think I started feeling it earlier than some because I've always felt one year older than I actually am. Maybe it's because I grew up with a man who likes to remind people that when they are thirty-nine, they are actually in their fortieth year. He's also the only one who points out that I'm developing age spots on my face. He can be quite charming.

Whatever the cause of my aging angst, I knew that at thirty-eight I'd feel thirty-nine, which gave me only one year until I felt forty. If I didn't get going on this dream now, when would it happen? Would I have to wait until life is less hectic and the kids are in college? Or at least until they are big enough to come with me? What if they hate hiking? What if social media, online gaming, and smartphones suck them into the vortex of self-loathing we hear so many teens suffer from these days? *Well, if that happens, I suppose I'll be hiking alone anyway.* But what if I don't make it another twenty years or another ten? I can't hike if I'm dead! And if I am lucky enough to live to retirement age, why should I wait until retirement to start doing what

I want to do now? For twenty years I'd been waiting to find the right time to climb, and I was finally realizing that there is no right time. The prospect of turning forty made me get serious about setting my goal in motion.

My intentions now out in the open, it was time to plan my first conquest. After letting the kids fill themselves up with the delicious crack butter from Texas Roadhouse, we drove home and I began some serious internet sleuthing. First, I consulted my favorite climbing website, Peakbagger.com, to get my list of forty-eight. Then I googled "the best" of every view, distance, trail and effort imaginable. The forty-eight presents a real conundrum because some of the shorter ones aren't necessarily easier to climb, and many of the peaks are best climbed with another one on the same day. Given that it was wintertime, and I didn't exactly know how much time was needed for each climb, I didn't know where to begin.

I settled upon Moosilauke because it stood by itself, eliminating the temptation to climb two mountains on my first effort. It was also the closest drive from my house, only two hours away. *Perfect*. This was January after all. Less time in the car meant more time for the trail. Time I was going to need since I was planning on carrying my skis. When I learned that Dartmouth hosted the first modern downhill ski race at Moosilauke in 1927, and its continuous stewardship still lures college-aged whippersnappers to backcountry ski its slopes, I couldn't resist. Thirty minutes of internet research was all it took to convince me that I too could climb up and ski down Moosilauke, like so many young bucks before me. *No problem!*

When I arrived at the closed gate, I was a little miffed about the extra mileage it added to the climb, but still too excited that I was actually out and doing this to let it stifle my enthusiasm. Fully geared up, I saw my shadow casting out before me, my skis pyramiding above my head, my hiking poles looking like weapons of the trail. I couldn't help but stop to admire how all of the equipment made my silhouette look like some rogue mountain warrior from a bygone era. Feeling pretty hardcore, I set off on a quick march, spurred forward by the sun and the bright blue sky.

The prospect of a long and great adventure before me triggered my senses. My eyes darted every which way, searching for views of the mountain, or perhaps a babbling brook. I started listening in earnest, and delighted in the sound of birch trees clapping their branches with the winter breeze. My wilderness rapture was only interrupted once, when I came across twelve Dartmouth students hiking back to their van, sleds in tow. *Sleds? College kids can't handle anything more than a few sleds?*

As they approached, I fantasized about all of the things they would say about the dude heading up the trail with skis on his back. "Who was that guy?" they'd say. "Did you see that twenty-something guy? I wonder what he's up to. Guy looks hardcore!" *No way would they guess that I am thirty-eight. No way!* After they passed, I looked back over my shoulder and noticed that none of them returned my gaze. The boys and girls were happily chatting with each other, oblivious to my presence, like four-year-olds with ice cream.

But I didn't need their affirmation. This was awesome. Venturing into the wild, I felt invigorated. My body had been craving a physical challenge beyond afternoon jogs and stints on the rowing machine. Modern exercise is a circle that takes you nowhere. Slapping your feet on the pavement, or taking in a Netflix show on the treadmill, can't rekindle those suppressed elements of your instinctual spirit that need to go outside into nature to feel alive. Like cells generating and re-generating in our bodies, we need to move out into the wilderness to regenerate our souls.

Trail signs confirmed I was heading in the right direction. The first one read "Path is STEEP & UNEVEN—Please Step Carefully." *Right on!* How disappointing would it be to arrive at a sign that said, "Path is FLAT and STRAIGHT"? Okay, so this first sign didn't offer a superior challenge, demanding grit and determination in the face of incredible odds, but at least it had an edgy vibe. *Bring on the steep path!*

The next sign I came across read: "Trail Closed. This Section of the Gorge Brook trail has been rerouted due to Water Damage. Please try our new Location a ¼ mile up the Snapper Trail. Thanks and Sorry for any inconvenience." *Nice Dartmouth kids.* Who else would give their apologies and such a thorough explanation, but an overanalytical college kid? Couldn't understand why random words were capitalized though. Maybe Dartmouth is a strong math Ivy.

Hearing about a little trail damage from Big Green did more than satisfy my curiosity; it also made me happy.

Exciting... damage! Signs noting problems or damage meant something for me to do. Something for me to work around and problem solve. Something to look back on and feel like I fought for something few others attempt. Later, freezing my ass off two hundred feet from the summit, I felt like I should be wearing a sign around my neck that said, "Grade A Moron."

Why do this to myself? *Why, why, why?* Why suffer the weight on my back, still bent on standing on the highest point of the mountain, conquering it, though neither man nor beast would be present to bear witness to my accomplishment? I've heard many climbers answer this question with the classic response, "because it was there," echoing George Mallory's comment regarding his climb up Mt. Everest. But this doesn't cut it. It's a cute reply for those that don't want to really explain themselves. It doesn't help anybody. "Because it was there" suggests that climbing is a mindless activity, comparable to eating or sleeping or relieving oneself. The physical and intellectual challenge for the common caveman. *Man eat. Man go bathroom. Man go climb. Left foot, right foot, left foot, uh, right foot. Man tired. Man go sleep now!*

Are there times on a climb when these physiological needs take over? Certainly. Are there times when you are so tired that your thoughts diminish to step counting? Absolutely. But what drives us to the mountains and the thoughts that carry us up their slopes are complicated and varied. They are for me at least. But who knows, maybe I'm sharing the trails with a bunch of mountain zombies.

Perhaps what Mallory was alluding to is a spiritual connection we feel for the mountains, which can only be understood by those who feel the need to ascend, so it wasn't worth answering more elaborately. Or perhaps he was tired from his climb and didn't feel like answering questions. Or maybe he wasn't much of a talker and in fact a surprisingly quite literal guy. The appeal of his statement is not its accuracy, but its vagueness, allowing the speaker to suggest deeper reasons of his own making without having to share what those are. When someone says, "because it was there," they may very well mean "because I was dealing with some serious shit I couldn't work out back home, and figured trudging up this giant hill would help."

Whatever leads you to the base of your mountain, the challenge before you shares similarities with regular life's challenges, whether that's getting a job, saving money for a house, or something else. When you set out to conquer your goal, you take the appropriate steps needed to get you to where you want to go, and during the course of your quest a variety of outcomes can occur. Sometimes you succeed without issue. Sometimes you get lost along the way and you have to double your efforts to reach your objective. Sometimes you fail completely.

But mountains are different and unique from anything else you will face in life in that they are the truest, cleanest representative of life's challenges in physical form. There is no mistaking the end goal, and there is no mistaking who got you there. You have to count on you, and your arrival at the summit is the simplest and most honest achievement for your soul that you can experience. No one else can lay claim to your accomplishment. No one else can soil it by saying they did it for you, or claim they did the same thing, unless they truly did the same thing, foot for foot, step for step. Others may help motivate you and encourage you along the way, but the two feet that actually did the lifting belong to you and you alone.

Climbing is a measurement of your physical and mental strength working together to take you into a tough area and then get yourself out. There are no shortcuts, except for the occasional butt sliding during a winter climb, but even that carries a risk/reward that is at its core, honest. Climbing is more honest than any human interaction you have ever had. The mountains have no hidden agendas and no lies to tell. They stand tall, daring you to take them on, making no apologies for being difficult or temperamental. This earns them your respect, and self-respect is what they give you in return for attempting their summits.

Before taking on my mission of the 4000-footers, I had climbed approximately a hundred mountains of various size. Some of the biggest ones were Kilimanjaro, Rainier, and Grand Teton's Enclosure, but many of them were under two thousand feet. No matter the height, all of them gave me a feeling of accomplishment and made many of life's problems seem smaller at their summits. That feeling lingers well after the climb and sustains you as you move forward in the real world, making you less afraid to meet challenges in work or school or in relationships. Some mountains trigger that feeling for weeks: in the case of Kilimanjaro, for me, it was years and years. Standing on top of a mountain that tested your body and spirit gives you the sense that there are adventures to be had in this life, and you are the kind of person that can have them. With forty lurking around the corner, I desperately wanted to find that feeling again.

Chapter 2

The Nudge

Following my failure at Moosilauke, I realized that I needed to get much smarter about planning each climb. From the start, Liz preached the importance of ascending multiple mountains on the same day if I was going to have a prayer in hell of summiting the 4000-footers before I turned forty, and the message was really starting to sink in. It had taken a very long day just to fail Moosilauke.

But Liz was generally referring to the big climbs, like the Presidential Traverse, where you can knock off eight mountains in a weekend. Or the Carter-Moriah Range, where you can maybe knock off six. Most of the climbs, however, are what I call "onesy-twosies," where you can only bag one peak per trip, two at best. Unfortunately (fortunately?) there are forty-eight of these suckers and the most efficient way to tackle them requires somewhere between twenty-five and thirty-five separate trips. There may be some nutbags out there reading this who say, "Not true Matt, you can do a Direttissima of all forty-eight!" That's where you climb all forty-eight in one continuous stretch of self-inflicted agony. To them I say, God love ya, and thank God for planting you on this earth so that any crazy idea I hatch sounds sensible to my wife. Keep it up.

Liz always knows people doing every kind of thing you can imagine, and before I could even accomplish one summit, she put feelers out to her extraordinary network of friends and co-conspirators to see who else was climbing the forty-eight. Within twenty-four hours she discovered some family friends from growing up—three young female athletes—who were attempting the feat over many years. Suddenly all I heard about was how these much, *MUCH* younger women had been working on their 4000-footers for years, and even though *THEY* were Olympic skiers, they still weren't done with climbing the forty-eight. In other words, Matt, you are delusional. And oh yeah, girls rule, boys drool.

Actually, Liz was simply emphasizing the planning process; she never expressed doubts about my ability to do it, though she certainly may have had them. When she trained me for the Boston Marathon, she thought I was a terrible pupil, and couldn't see how I was going to convert my smattering of training runs into a successful race. My longest training run was eighteen miles, which I decided was good enough, and that I could wing the rest of it come go-time. My dad, never the casual observer, found it amusing to watch Liz get exasperated over my regimen. "She's learning" he said. "You just kind of do what you're gonna do." Truth be told, I didn't think I had it in me to do more than one eighteen-mile run, and I didn't want to use it up on a training effort. Liz thought I was out of my tree.

But despite her doubts about my style, Liz champions my efforts. During the marathon she managed to take our kids and intercept me at not one, not two, but *three* different spots along the race in order to cheer me on, complete with handwritten signs. I think that's more impressive than me running it. When I saw her at mile seventeen, I was crashing hard and had to walk for a few minutes. She put her arm around me and told me how proud she was of me. All I kept thinking was, *How the heck did you do four of these?* Then she met me at the finish line, dragging our kids all the way, providing smiles to fill me up.

It was only fitting then that after my Moosilauke disappointment, and hardly a single hike in the ten months that followed, Liz suggested we go climbing one weekend to get the ball rolling for me. Life with kids had pulled us in a million directions over the past year and we were needing some "us time," so we headed to the White Mountains for the weekend. Reading up on the forty-eight in the months prior, I thought we should probably start with a smaller peak like Cannon, but Liz had different ideas and suggested we finish what I started on Moosilauke instead. *What a gal!*

It was a beautiful November day, and as we headed up Route 93, New Hampshire's gateway to the mountains, we were excited about the prospect of beginning this adventure together. The weather was mild and with no snow on the ground I assumed we could pull right up to the base of the mountain, clipping off the additional mileage I had to hike last time. But when we took Exit 32 and turned right towards the town of Woodstock, a sinking feeling came over me that the access road wouldn't be open. I never bothered to check its status online. Sure enough, when we turned up the entry road, we discovered that the gate was indeed already closed for the season. "Okay, so we just walk farther," Liz said. If I was alone, I would have had the same thought, but I wasn't expecting Liz to react so well to another round of poor planning. Stepping out of the car, I gave myself a mental high-five for marrying correctly.

Outside, the air was cool. A gentle breeze tickled my ears, but it was sunny and comfortable—good hiking weather. Two guys who looked like they could be snapped apart for kindling were at the sedans next to us, saddling up with running backpacks. Greeting each other cordially, they admired each other's gear with false enthusiasm, signaling that outside of their hobby, they might not have much to say to each other. Or maybe they hadn't eaten enough protein yet to venture into more robust discussion topics. I checked our packs to make sure we had enough food and then, donning hats and gloves, we set off at a brisk pace.

Within minutes I was sweating like a polar bear on the equator. Off came the hat, the gloves, my jacket, and my fleece. I like to think I heat up so quickly because of my

Norwegian Viking blood, inherited from my great-grandfather Lars Larson. It may only account for an eighth of me, but I choose to believe it rules the other seven-eighths with an iron fist and a hammer.

Following the same Gorge Brook Trail I skied ten months earlier, we stopped along the way to enjoy the views of other mountains and wonder which ones they were. I also pondered some of the plants we saw. I've always wanted to learn more about botany but never found the time. I'm not a birder, but I find looking up bird types to be a more gratifying exercise than looking up plants. Bird markings are more distinct and you can usually narrow down what you saw when consulting the web. *Ah yes, that bird that tried to steal my food on vacation in Florida was a grackle. I think.*

With no skis on our backs, we made good time. What was a long and arduous day in January was a simple hike in November, taking no more than a few hours to get to the same spot where I had turned back before. How embarrassing. With a clear sky and dry trails, I could now see how ridiculously close to the summit I had been. Definitely not more than a couple hundred feet of elevation gain, and literally a fifteen-minute walk up for me and Liz. I pushed my frustration down into the pit of my stomach and smiled in disbelief. "You gotta be kidding me."

The summit of Moosilauke is open and splendid. On a November day it can appear rather brown, as do most places in New Hampshire at that time of year, but the summit expanse allows you to have an unimpeded view of the surrounding range, aided by the fact it stands higher than any of the western White Mountains. For weekend warriors from Boston and the burbs, it's one of the quickest 4000-footers to get to and the likely explanation for the crowd before us, sipping on Gatorade and chomping on trail mix.

Most of the climbers were middle-aged men wearing baby-blue Patagonia jackets, and we asked one to take our picture at the summit sign. Moosilauke has these bright orange signs that give a little energy to the hike and make for great photographs. After he snapped a couple photos for us, I asked if we could return the favor. "No, no," he said. "I've already got my forty-eight under my belt. No picture needed." *Well, well, well, look at you.* Informed of his superiority, I returned to my lunch without further comment.

After a few minutes of repose, the sweat running down my back gave me a chill and I needed to bundle up. Liz, having only shed her hat on the ascent, now threw it back on. We started to fantasize about a warm dinner by the fireplace at the Common Man restaurant in Lincoln and took that as our cue to leave. Proceeding down the Carriage Road Trail, built for horse carriages in the 1800s, we were glad to have the option of taking a different route back to our car. Loop trails help break up the tedium by giving you something new to look at.

On the descent we fell in line with a tall woman who was feverishly trying to gain distance on us but failing, much to her chagrin. Hiking too closely to be ignored, Liz struck up a conversation and within minutes discovered that she knew people the woman worked with. It's uncanny. We could be in the middle of Zimbabwe and Liz would be able to make a connection with someone who knows the same people. Now at ease, the woman mentioned she was in grad school and loves coming up to the mountains to clear her head.

"Where do you go to school?" Liz asked.

"Oh, in Boston," the lady replied.

"Where in Boston?"

"Cambridge?"

"Oh, you mean Harvard?" Liz and I said in unison, chuckling. Why do Harvard people do this? Does Harvard have some weird orientation program where they tell their students that because they are at the most prestigious college in the country, they should try to act humble and never tell anyone where they go to school? *Be more discreet,* they say, *tell them you go to school in Boston.* It's not as painful as the Princeton grad who manages to mention their upcoming reunion in every conversation possible, but someone should tell Harvard people that it's okay for them to say that they go to Harvard the first time they are asked.

But I digress. Tired of our banter, the Harvard gazelle accelerated her pace, and we eventually slowed ours, catching the drift that she wanted to be alone. I couldn't blame her. Everyone needs their space, and the mountains are one of the greatest places to go and get some distance from our fellow man. I too have begrudged many a soul that came marching up an isolated trail with their noise and conversation, inanely laughing about nothing at all.

Sometimes these sounds are welcome, and sometimes they can make me feel quite grinchy.

Liz and I love to hike in both talk and quiet mode. On this day, while not the loudest pair of hikers, we were happily chatting away. It was our first chance to get away together for quite some time, and it had us excited. I was also thrilled to have my Moosilauke failure addressed and thankful that Liz got me going again. We spent the time talking about our kids, soaking up the scenery, and joking about life. Once we got back to the car, we made haste for some beer and wine in front of a roaring fire, which every climber knows is the finest way to finish a grand day in the mountains. It was a wonderfully misleading way to officially begin my adventure.

Chapter 3

Spikeless

My hand woke before my head and fumbled its way around in the dark for the snooze button, knocking pens and books to the floor before finding its mark. Somehow, Liz slept through the ruckus. It was 4am, and even though I was buried under a couple of blankets, I could feel the cold seeping its way through our bedroom windows, warning me to stay indoors. My body begged me to keep sleeping, and I almost yielded, but then a voice from deep within forced my eyes to crack open. It said, "Come on, get up."

Following the successful ascent of the Moose, I finally outlined a proper plan of attack for completing the forty-eight. During the winter I was going to knock off as many "onesy-twosies" as I could, before tackling some larger groupings in the summer months. I wrote down the names of every mountain and researched the plot map off

Peakbagger.com to see which ones I could combine into reasonable groupings. I did this knowing full well that plans could and would change. But putting a plan down on paper helped me get my mind right and gave birth to the voice within that wouldn't let me sleep in anymore.

It always takes me about thirty minutes to really wake up. I'm a chronic allergy sufferer and most mornings it feels like my eyes are welded shut. My eyes are prone to getting bloodshot and allergies often have me feeling dried out, especially during the winter when the furnace cranks up and kicks out a bunch of dust. My throat gets scratchy, my eyes get sticky, and the fog in my head doesn't lift for an hour. Coffee helps at times, but it gives me the shakes. Even decaf. So I try to avoid it unless I am desperate. Ironically, Red Bull, laced with taurine and caffeine and whatever other "ines" they have in there, is a more naturally pleasing substitute. A can of it was waiting for me in the truck in case I couldn't keep my eyes open.

Turns out rolling along in the dark, the anticipation of getting out there again, was all the stimulant I needed. It wasn't the thrill of the climb that snapped me awake, but knowing that I was heading back to the place where I first remember feeling profound love. Oh, how I do love the White Mountains. For so long I had waited to fully explore them, and I couldn't believe it was finally happening. They hold a certain magic for me and, quite simply, have always made me feel better about life.

When I was a kid growing up in Massachusetts, my parents used to take me skiing at Loon Mountain. Leaving the stop and go traffic of Boston, crossing the border into

New Hampshire, I always started to feel happier. There was something about catching that first glimpse of the mountains while traveling up Route 93 that made me feel like I was going home. The closer we got to Exit 32, the happier I felt. Everything was better up there: the air was cleaner, the people were nicer, the scenery was prettier, the pace was slower. Leaving hectic Massachusetts behind, where everyone seemed hellbent on keeping up with the Jones's, I felt the contrast deeply. Loon was also my favorite place to be with my parents because they would finally get to relax, relieved from the stress of work and regular life. At Loon we could be ourselves, unfettered and unplanned.

Liz and I moved to New Hampshire in 2004 to work at Fidelity Investments in Merrimack, but we both left our jobs there years ago and are free to go wherever we want. We've played with the idea of moving back to Massachusetts numerous times, in order to be closer to our families, but we always talk ourselves out of it: we can't find anything more suitable for our family than our little town of Amherst. It's perfect for us. Besides, we want to spend all of our weekends outside skiing, hiking, and exploring: why move an hour and a half in the wrong direction to pay three times more for a house and spend half my life in traffic? Makes no sense. If anything, I want to move closer to the mountains, not farther away from them.

My plan for the day was to bag two peaks—Osceola and East Osceola—not out of a need to take a chunk out of the list, but because I wanted to expedite my relationship with the forty-eight. With only one mountain under my belt so far, I was anxious to immerse myself in this experience and believed that the only way I could achieve that was through volume. The Greeley Ponds Trailhead, located off the Kancamagus Highway in Lincoln, was the launchpad for East Osceola and only forty minutes from where I needed to be for work that afternoon, so I figured I could take advantage of the drive north to nab a couple of mountains before my meetings. I am nothing if not optimistic.

Taking good old Exit 32 off Route 93 again, I couldn't believe that the starting point for yet another 4000-footer was so close to where I grew up skiing as a kid. I also couldn't believe it when somebody pulled in right behind me at the trailhead. *Who the heck could this be?* Judging that nobody sane could be out at this hour, the irony was completely lost on me.

Out of our cars, gearing up, we made small talk about how it should be a good day for a climb. I was playing it cool, chatting about the weather and how nice it is to get out, but on the inside I was starting to panic that this guy knew something I didn't. I mean, who shows up at the predawn hour to climb a mountain in the middle of winter? *Alone?* Certainly not a novice. Probably in his early sixties and relatively fit despite having a bit of a potbelly, nothing about his person indicated "expert mountaineer." He did, however, look way more prepared than me. As he readied his pack, I took note of the following: hiking poles, several wick-away shirts, multiple layers to protect himself from the elements, and what sounded like a bag of chains.

"Looks like a good day for spikes," he cheerily proclaimed.

Not wanting to reveal my ignorance, I promptly replied "Right!"

When a hiker says, "spikes," I later learned, they are referring to microspikes or crampons, which are the two main forms of adding metal-toothed traction to your boots. Adding traction keeps you from slipping on the ice as you climb and can help save you a lot of time. Crampons are the more traditional type of traction, which require you to wear a special type of boot so that a crampon can lock onto it, or "cramp on." The newer microspikes, on the other hand, can be slipped right over your regular hiking boots. Presto. No special boot purchase required. Microspikes are a trendy acquisition in the winter hiking world, which I still knew absolutely nothing about. I didn't have microspikes or crampons; I was spikeless.

What I did have was something called Yaktrax, which, like microspikes, fit over your boot, but provide a lot less traction. Made of rubber straps and laced with metal rings, they are essentially snow tires for your feet. I had tried them out plenty of times before and they had worked great, but that was on flat hiking trails or while shoveling the driveway. I knew that I should have something better than Yaktrax for the task at hand, but I didn't know exactly what yet.

Spikeman left me to ponder these mysteries of winter climbing. By the time I got my act together, he was long gone, but that was okay by me. His presence had thrown my expectations of intended solitude for a loop and now that I was peacefully alone, the morning could be reclaimed. I loved breathing in the cold fresh air and listening to the sounds of the woods, uninterrupted by human interference. The illusion of controlled circumstances provided me space to let go, and mindlessly, I happily ambled my way up the trail.

Thirty minutes later my parking lot compadre came welcomingly back into view. He had paused by the side of the trail to get his spikes out, but I didn't bother to inspect them as I passed by. Large patches of ice interposed the middle of the trail here, forcing me to the sides to find good dirt to tread on. Soon the trail was more ice than dirt, and I had to hop my way around like Indiana Jones tiptoeing past booby traps to get the Golden Idol. When fancy footwork wasn't enough, I grabbed trees to keep my balance. Falling felt imminent. I don't know why I kept trying to proceed this way, well past the point of needing traction. Maybe it was because my subconscious knew something I didn't. Finally, after one leg slipped uncomfortably outward on the ice, I went into my pack to retrieve the Yaktrax, only to discover that I had left them in the car. *You gotta be kidding me.* Only my second mountain and I was unprepared, yet again. *What the hell is wrong with me?*

Spikeman motored up to me while I continued to search my pack. He asked if I was doing okay, to which I sheepishly glanced up and said, "I left my spikes in the car." *Your not-spikes, you mean.* He was sympathetic but said something about how at least I got out there, and then rocketed up the hill. With spikes he was moving four times as fast and disappeared from sight in short order. *At least I got out here?* Determined to move on, I grabbed my pack and followed after him.

Using trees to pull myself along, I wasn't breaking any records, but I started feeling confident that this was all doable. Slow, but doable. That is until I arrived at an open rock face pitched at a sixty-degree angle, covered in sheer ice. Venturing the tiniest of steps forward to test it out, I slipped and fell right away, my ass hitting the ground. Hard. Propping myself up against a large boulder to recover my senses and my pride, I let out a deep breath. *What now? How the hell am I going to navigate this?* Hoping some sustenance would inspire creativity, I snapped into an energy bar, but all my thoughts swirled around the idea that if I was to fail summitting every mountain before successfully climbing it, this was going to be a much longer and humiliating journey than I had anticipated. When the energy bar was gone, I started munching on a peanut butter and jelly sandwich.

While contemplating a call to Liz to inform her what a dufus she married, two young men came marching up the path. One of them was talking a million miles a minute, exuberantly describing his last climb, his buddy patiently absorbing every word. They emerged on the rock face, and I immediately noticed that they weren't wearing any spikes. A tiny candle flickered in my stomach. If they were able to proceed without spikes, maybe I could too.

"Hey man, how you doing?" the loud one greeted me.

"Well, okay, except I forgot my spikes." *Let's get right to it.*

"Oh no! What a bummer! I just got these the other day and they are awesome!" He took out a pair of red microspikes and began strapping them on. Gesturing at his friend, he said, "I was telling him, these are the best things ever. Best new invention for hiking in winter. You climbing the 4000-footers?"

"Yeah, you?"

"Yeah, this will be number seven and eight for me. I am psyched to do the chimney. That looks rad." I had no idea what the chimney was.

"Six and seven for me," said the friend.

"How about you?" chatterbox asked.

"Well, I've done a few before but I'm starting them over, so this was supposed to be my second and third, but it's not looking good."

I watched with envy as they laid their spikes on the ground, stretched the rubber straps over the toes and heels of their boots, and then pulled the spikes snug to the soles. They worked exactly like the Yaktrax I didn't have. I had never seen them before and didn't realize how easy they would be to manage; it was a certainty that I would be buying them before my next climb. After wishing me good luck, the fearless duo moseyed their way up the open rock face with little trouble, an impressively depressing sight.

That sealed it. Taking the last bites of my PB&J, I decided that I was going to have to go down when two college kids appeared—a couple, it seemed. They were slipping and sliding all over the place and the girl looked worried. The boy seemed not to care. After she confirmed that they too were spikeless, I voiced my concerns about going any further, and told her I was planning on turning back. She agreed that maybe they should do the same.

Not acknowledging me or my advice, the boy attempted the open rock face in some flats normally reserved for urbanites ready to do some serious street walking. He managed to climb ten feet until he was standing on a tiny dry patch of rock, no bigger than a single square foot. Standing there with those stupid little shoes, completely surrounded by ice and having no ability to ascend any further, I realized that I was no longer the dumbest person on the mountain. I considered telling the girl to dump him on the spot.

Something about that boy made the idea of coming so close and failing again too much to bear, and I decided to ascend after all. But climbing up the rock face without spikes was not only foolish, it was dangerous. Much better, I thought, to hoist myself up through the bramble and get stabbed by a thousand tree branches than risk falling on some ice and hurtling off the mountainside. One easy slip could send you down fifty feet or more.

Hucking the remnants of my lunch into my pack, I announced my plans to the girl and took a few cautious steps. It was only about eight feet to the trees on the other side of the trail, but I slipped again, this time uncomfortably close to the edge of the cliff. As my kids would say, this got me triggered. Frustration surging, feet slipping in opposite directions, I lunged across the gap and managed to grasp a skinny young pine, which I used like a rope to pull me over to the treeline. *Yes!* It probably didn't look all that dramatic to someone else, but I was pretty sure the move defied physics. Upon my success, the girl told her boyfriend that she was following me, and he offered her a quiet grunt in reply. Eventually he followed as well.

Once I was safely embedded among the tightly knit trees, I slowly worked my way up the slope, breaking through branches and finding tiny gaps to stand where there was enough ground to place my feet. What seemed an impossible task only moments ago was proving solvable. I endured a few scrapes on my arms here and there, but the workaround wasn't bad, and after a few minutes I was on the topside of the rock face, back on the regular trail. It was icy here as well, but at least you could find dirt to stand on again, and there were plenty of trees for support when you couldn't. Before long, I was standing at the summit of East Osceola where I was warmly greeted by Spikeman and the two young men in love with their microspikes.

"You made it," Spikeman said, with a smile. He looked genuinely pleased I persevered.

"Yep, I did!"

"You going to keep going?"

"Let me take a look," I said, pointing down the trail that would take me to Osceola "proper." Twenty yards away, the trail dropped down into what I surmised was the "chimney" that my chatty buddy was referring to. Whatever it was, it looked hairy: a perilous staircase of granite, completely encased in ice, with no trees to grab or dirt to stand on. It was a deathtrap. If I was lucky enough to survive it, there was also the issue of time. Sans spikes, I was moving slowly, and I needed to get to work. If I attempted the chimney, wherever it was, who knows how long it would be before I got back to my car. Grateful to have bagged one peak, I headed back towards my new friends and told them that this was it for me today. "I'm out." Past experience made this an easy decision.

Chapter 4

The Lonely Backpack

Long before I started having my mid-life crisis, I had my third decade crisis, in which I convinced my brother-in-law Justin and my buddy Jonathan to head to Wyoming with me in order to tackle the Grand Teton. Liz and her sister Margaret (Justin's wife) had already climbed it years earlier, and I figured it was high time Justin and I got ours. Jonathan, always up for an athletic challenge, was the perfect wingman to complete our triumvirate. Justin and Jonathan didn't know each other at the time, but my gut told me that they would be a good fit.

Even though I had spent more time in the mountains than them, I was definitely the least athletic of the three. At five-foot-nine, with a little paunch belly and stout physique, I was more muscle than fat, but you could say my ratios could have been a bit better. Justin on the other hand was tall and lean, a former collegiate swimmer and baseball pitcher. He did triathlons for fun. Jonathan was even more of a lunatic, with hopes of completing a marathon in every state, and maintaining a healthy eating regimen that only Tom Brady would approve of. Intense, I know. And exactly my kind of guys. Except for the healthy eating part. Give me the ice cream and nobody gets hurt.

I specifically asked these two to join me because I knew Grand Teton was going to be hard. It requires strong mental focus while expending an extraordinary amount of physical energy. Guys who were willing to put themselves through triathlons and marathons on a regular basis were more inclined to see this as a fun challenge. And it didn't hurt that they are fun to hang out with as well.

Since Grand Teton requires some technical climbing, we didn't want to screw around, so we chose to go with Exum Mountain Guides out of Jackson, Wyoming, to help us get to the top. Exum's ascent schedule called for two days of training, followed by a two-day climb to the summit, and we couldn't wait to get going. Of all the groups attempting to summit, we were the youngest, strongest group, and noting our excitement, they decided to hook us up with a gung-ho psychopath for a guide that the other guides dubbed "The Masochist."

The first day of training was great. We practiced belaying and repelling over some cliff edges. We worked on our footwork and learned how to trust each other on the ropes. Our guide didn't seem so bad after all, and we spent part of the morning relaxing, enjoying nature and the sun, talking about the beauty of the mountains and such. Everything seemed alright. Then day two happened.

Evidently pleased with our Day 1 efforts, the Masochist came alive. Feeling like we could attempt a more difficult ascent of Grand Teton, he wanted to see what we were made of and pushed us hard up some really scary shit. He frequently yelled at us to "be careful" and "hurry up," the mixed messages dripping with annoyance and stress. The barrage of commands made me lose my concentration a few times while I was belaying the ropes, which genuinely freaked me out.

Hundreds of feet below us I could see one of the other climbing groups, laughing and taking their time, enjoying the day and heading up a significantly easier route. That looked nice. Meanwhile the Masochist kept telling us that if we weren't careful, we were going to die. As we worked the ropes and looked for holds, he kept shouting things down to us like, "Keep moving guys. Good movement is the difference between life and death," and "you make a mistake up here, you're going to die." Down below I could hear another guide telling a woman in her 50s, "you're doing great." The other guides had warned us, and now we believed them. This guy was crazy.

Still, the three of us kept up with every demand he threw at us. For three inexperienced technical climbers, we made several solid ascents of some very tough stuff. I frequently found myself standing on a tiny crack, barely large enough to fit my big toe on, with nothing but two fingers holding me close to the mountain face. Pushing off my big toe I'd find another crack to step on and then reach up for the next two-fingered hold. This went on for hours and we did it all while schlepping thirty-pound packs on our backs. We were killing it.

When we got to the hardest challenge of the day, I was feeling pretty good. And strong. The last technical ascent involved an enormous cliff, where after climbing more than four hundred feet, you came underneath a round precipice you had to climb up and over. It looked impossible unless you were Alex Honnold. But I trusted the steps our guide taught me, drove my hiking shoes into the rock face, and used my fingers to lift myself up. I did it and I was stoked. As a rule, I never use the word stoked, but here I was, feeling it. Thrilled about our collective success on climbing such a terrifying wall of rock, I believed we were surely destined for something truly epic on the summit climb, but as I tried to take a step forward, my enthusiasm was halted. I couldn't budge.

Thirty feet below me, Justin, the anchor of our rope team, gave me a quizzical look. "I can't move—the rope is stuck," I shouted. Above me, standing on a cropping of rocks fifty degrees to my right, the Masochist paced back and forth like a cougar waiting for its supper. We made eye contact and he asked me what the holdup was. When I told him the rope was stuck on some rock down below and that I couldn't move, his face flared with anger and he shouted, "Go back then! Go back down. Come on Matt!" My eyes bulged. *Go back?* There was nothing to hold onto if I went back down. No place for my feet. Nothing but sky and a few hundred feet. Maybe five hundred. *Is he nuts?* I looked up at Jonathan who was leading the rope team, and his eyes were bulging too. He lifted one hand in the air and shook his head as if to say, "Holy shit man, I have no idea." I think we were both scared.

Fearing the wrath of our guide more than death, and not wanting to let the group down, I began my descent over the cliff wall. Laying down on my stomach, I shimmied towards the edge as the Masochist bawled me out. What he was saying, I couldn't tell you; my mind was trying to concentrate on not falling off the mountain. Time warped as I dropped my feet over the cliff's edge and felt nothing but air. It was the only time I've ever been one hundred percent, completely and utterly terrified while climbing.

I don't know about you, but when my legs are dangling over a cliff, my instinct is to pull myself up, not follow my feet. It felt like I was hanging off the side of the Hancock Tower. Trying not to think about it, I kept moving. I had faith in Jonathan, and knew I was tied on, so I used all the arm strength I had to reach me and my pack down over the rock face. As my arms dropped myself downward, I swung my feet forty-five degrees towards the mountain in hopes that I'd hit some kind of stone ledge I could get a foothold on. I did. It was a bloody freaking miracle.

Later, after re-ascending that same damn cliff and reflecting on the day's events, all of us agreed that we had signed up with the wrong cowboy. But it was too late. All the other guides were committed to other groups, so we had to stick it out with Psycho if we wanted to climb the Grand. One thing was clear though—if we got stranded on the mountain without any food or water, there was no question who we were going to eat first.

The first day of the ascent up Grand Teton turned out to be wonderful. We hiked through fields of sunflowers and asters, enjoyed a great deal of sun, and drank from a natural spring that popped up through the rocks along the side of the trail. Psycho was in a good mood and we mostly forgot he was there, despite his constant reminders that we could die at any moment. Eventually we moved from summer to winter and came to camp on the lower saddle, situated at an elevation of 11,600 feet. Grand Teton's summit is at 13,776 feet, so after a long day of climbing, the saddle is the customary place to hit the sack. It was lights out by 8:30 because at 3:30 the next morning we were going to go for the summit.

Waking in the dark to start a mountain climb is an experience like no other, and one I highly recommend you do at some point in your life. Despite the early hour, your senses swiftly come alive as you wonder about the adventure ahead. Gathering by the packs to check our gear, everyone speaks quietly and sparingly so not to wake any of the climbers who are hoping for a later start. Besides the sounds of crunching granola and coffee being slurped, not much can be heard but the sounds of zippers and scuffling nylon. We were the first group up and after Psycho did a final rope check, he gave us a nod and we were off.

Psycho wanted to get off to a quick start in order to get out ahead of the other groups, so we hustled out of camp at a quick clip. After making our way in the dark for thirty minutes, we could see the headlamps of the other climbers bobbing up and down on the trail far below us like little fireflies in the night. Given their pace during the previous days of climbing, we knew there was little risk of them catching up to us, which helped ease Psycho's intensity level. He took his foot off the gas, allowing us to slow down and climb in more relative peace.

For the first hour of climbing, I couldn't see any of the surrounding valley or the mountain ahead; only the four or five moves ahead of me as we scrambled over the rocks illuminated by our headlamps. But as we made our way to the upper saddle, I could start to make out the valley below in the early morning shadows and realized that inches below the narrow space where my left foot was standing, was a sheer drop of what looked like hundreds of feet. Maybe a thousand. *What the hell?* I spoke to Jonathan who was a few steps ahead of me. "Do you see how narrow this trail is?" Jonathan, a new father of only a couple months, expressed the first real sounds of caution I had heard from him. "Let's be careful."

When we finally stopped for a rest, we shared our disbelief that we hadn't roped in for that section of the climb. Hand over hand climbing in the dark, stepping along a narrow path on the edge of a cliff, seemed like exactly the right time for us to rope in. The Masochist overheard us, despite our best efforts to speak in hushed tones, and told us that "if one of us fell on that section there was no sense in all of us dying from one guy taking a slip." It felt like that possibility was something we should have discussed beforehand.

Shockingly, Admiral Death-March was relatively quiet during the ascent to the upper saddle, resisting the urge to inform us of the mortal peril we were in and failing to utter any snarling commands. In fact, he was mildly complimentary of our pace and effort. What was quite audible though was the ceaseless rain, which peppered us mercilessly the entire trek. By the time we made it to the top of the upper saddle we were drenched, and the heavy winds steadily beating against our shoulders indicated that a letup wasn't coming.

Below us we could make out that some, if not all of the groups behind us, were turning back. Rather than being alarmed by this, I stopped minding the rain so much. But then we overtook a guide and two young climbers who had surprisingly managed to sneak out of camp before us. Soaked to the bone, they were contemplating turning back when we passed them by. The young men looked particularly run through, expressionless and cold, ready to call it a day. But the guide looked whooped as well, and perhaps a little bit worried. This gave me pause.

Not wanting to waste any more time, we raced towards an enormous boulder that was sitting right under the final technical ascent of the Grand, hoping it would offer us a reprieve from the deluge. It didn't. We were totally exposed and as the sky grew evermore ominous, some initial thoughts of doubt passed our minds. Surveying the area and each other, we noted that the young climbers were now descending, officially making us the last group still trying to ascend. Not ready to face the meaning of this, my eyes gravitated back to the boulder as I scanned the earth, and my brain, for a solution to our predicament. What I found was a backpack.

Wedged under a crevice where the boulder met the ground was an ordinary blue backpack, evidently stuffed with a fair amount of climbing gear. The final few hundred feet to Grand Teton's summit are technical and exactly what our rope training was intended for; it felt strange for a pack filled with climbing gear to be left behind at the most critical spot. Given the heavy rains, this last wall was going to be particularly sketchy, with a ton of slick vertical rock to navigate. The presence of the lonely backpack didn't make any sense at all and kind of gave me the willies. *Who did it belong to? Did they leave it to carry less weight for the final ascent, or did something go awry? Is this some kind of sign?*

The Grim Reaper, who had been foretelling death at every turn for most of the adventure, now did a full 180 and prodded us forward, not finding the presence of the abandoned backpack foreboding in the slightest. Justin and I wanted to proceed, mainly because our wives had climbed Grand Teton a few years earlier; we were simultaneously jealous and determined to reclaim dignity for the male species. But Jonathan's new fatherhood was weighing on him, and he expressed some growing concern. He kept saying, "I don't know fellas." Being a father myself, I supposed that I should probably exercise similar caution. *But* . . .

I tried to be optimistic and thought I saw a break in the distant clouds, so I suggested we wait for ten minutes and see if the break grew large enough to push the rain away. Fifteen minutes later, no such luck was occurring. The skies were downright gloomy, and the rain pelted us a little harder than before. "We going to do it?" Psycho asked. I already knew the answer was going to be no, but hearing Psycho's willingness, while recalling his complete lack of normal behavior in the previous days, led me to conclude that his brand of optimism should not be followed. It made it easier for me to agree with what happened next.

I looked at Jonathan and he said, "Sorry guys, but it's a no for me." Justin and I both wished he had said the opposite, but we knew he was right. Slowly, painfully, we made the decision to turn back. It felt like the final decision was put in my hands and I said something like, "Okay, that's it. We're with you." Suddenly Psycho was totally cool and said, "That's okay guys, that's what you do up here. You make these decisions as a team. I think if you guys want, we can still safely climb to the summit of The Enclosure, which is the location of an old Indian site and is pretty cool." We all jumped at that idea and readied our packs. Before debarking, Psycho had us film a little explanation of our situation and I gave a rundown of the events. None of us spoke too much about the lonely backpack, but it was unquestionably the single biggest factor in our decision-making process to leave.

Up there in the clouds, making such choices can be tough. You've come a great distance, taken a plane flight, and worked your tail off to get oh so close. Turning back is not an option you ever considered when you made your initial plan to grab a peak. But when you're in the thick of it, you have to listen to the concerns of your team and make a group decision that will keep everyone safe. Jonathan's gut steered us away from the summit, and his decision became our decision. I knew it was the right one, but I didn't like it. Hell, Jonathan didn't like it. But it turned out that the best two decisions we made on the entire trip were listening to Jonathan and inviting him to come along in the first place.

After successfully summiting the Enclosure, we returned to high camp on the lower saddle, where word came in that a climber was missing. We were the only ones who had seen the backpack and after we notified the rangers in charge, a rescue effort was immediately put together. No time to rest, Psycho guided us down some glacial terrain before heading back up to join the search. As he took his leave of us, he felt it necessary to say that he "had doubts" about my abilities before today, but then conceded that me and the fellas did well. We watched him rapidly ascend the rock and snow, all of us impressed with how quickly he made time. He was the worst.

We descended the rest of the mountain on our own, reaching the trailhead a little before sunset. Soaked and battered, but pleased we had a major summit under our belts, we were three dudes who had successfully battled the elements. The weather had been raw, to say the least, and that was enough to make me feel like a stud for the moment. When we collected our climbing certificates from Exum, they informed us that we climbed higher than anyone else in the state of Wyoming that day—the weather had turned everyone else back. *Hell yeah.* I enjoyed hearing that.

That night we slept like the dead. When we woke, we spent an easy day recuperating, avoiding the elephant in the lodge. It wasn't until dinner that we were finally willing to discuss the decision. Jonathan felt terrible about it and kept apologizing, but Justin and I did our best to reiterate that it was the right call, and that he shouldn't beat himself up over it. It had little effect. The decision to turn back wasn't going to sit well with any of us for a while, but I was starting to feel okay about it. We still climbed a damn big peak and got to have an epic guys' trip that didn't result in our guide killing us. We were alive, right? That's a bonus. In fact, I was beginning to feel pretty good about the whole thing.

The next morning, while waiting for our plane to take off, I picked up a copy of the *Jackson Hole Daily*. On the cover was an article titled "Rangers Recover Body From Canyon." Turned out that the owner of the backpack had slipped off some rocks thirty or forty feet above where we were standing and fell 2,500 feet down into Valhalla canyon. Some later reports said 4,000 feet from where we were, but I can't find any geographical proof to support that. "Well, Jonathan, it looks like you made the right call," I said, handing him the paper. I no longer had any doubts.

On every big mountain climb I've done, someone has either died while I was climbing it or died right before we headed out. It happened at Kilimanjaro. It happened at Rainier. It happened at Grand Teton. We need adventure to feel alive, to feel free, but it's important to be "controlled wild" in our adventures, which is to say, wild but careful. Dangerous conditions present themselves at 13,000 feet and 4,000 feet alike, so I didn't lose any sleep over my failure to summit Osceola. I'd rather live to climb another day.

What struck me the most about the climber who fell into Valhalla was not the fall, or that he died, but that he was climbing alone and without any ropes. Without ropes to catch you and friends to confer with, poor decisions can lead to fatal mistakes in situations where there is no room for error. Hopefully you are lucky enough to have pals who want to do some crazy shit with you in this life, but the guts to let the mountain go when the risk isn't worth the price.

Chapter 5

Wogging

My exploits to date had proven that I was as likely to fail as succeed on my summit attempts, and something needed to change. I decided what I needed most was to step up my preparation game. Starting this mission in the wintertime was proving to be quite humbling, but summiting East Osceola without any spikes was also encouraging; it got me thinking that winter climbing won't be so hard as long as I do in fact, get spikes. A trip to Eastern Mountain Sports was in order.

If you're from New England and haven't heard of Eastern Mountain Sports, or "EMS," you've been living under a rock. In my work travels I frequently passed by two of them—one in Nashua on the Daniel Webster Highway, and one in Hingham, Massachusetts, nestled in among the wealthy elite. But there was no way I was going to spend my money in the Hingham store. I love the idea of earning money in Massachusetts and then spending it back in New Hampshire, doing what I can to support the war effort against our southern neighbor. Plus, there's no sales tax in New Hampshire, so it's always cheaper to buy in the Granite State. Live free or die, baby!

Within seconds of entering EMS I found some Kahtoola microspikes, which looked exactly like the ones my loud friend on East Osceola had recommended. *Done and done.* But making my way to the checkout counter was not so easy. Spikes in hand, I couldn't stop eyeballing all the other goodies in the store: Smartwool socks, crampons, tents, carabiners, ice screws, headlamps, compasses, jackets—I wanted all of them. I didn't know what I'd do with ice screws but I sure as heck wanted to take them home, spread them out on the dining room table, and imagine all of the cool things I could do with them. The gear greed was real.

The most alluring equipment was a pair of Black Diamond leather gloves, colored construction glove yellow with black trim and designed to withstand rugged use in cold temperatures. *Perfect*, I thought, until I saw the $110 price tag. After a minor coronary, I turned my attention towards the ice axes. *Do I need an ice axe?* I wanted to need one. But they were over a hundred dollars as well. Feeling a little gun-shy, I told myself that the ice axe would be the next purchase, should the trail conditions warrant it. They eventually would and I bought the ice axe the following week. The week after that I got the gloves.

Better equipped, it was time to up my internet search game. If I was going to improve my success rate, I needed to know more about the actual mountains I was climbing before I climbed them. Previously I had settled upon the Osceola peaks because they were among the closest mountains to my house. Now I realized how short-sighted it was to plan that way. If there were easier winter climbs a little farther down the road, I could save myself a boatload of time and reduce my risk of getting hurt. After seeing so many people on Osceola fighting the elements, I knew somebody had to be blogging about winter climbing the forty-eight, so I turned to the internet for a consult. Hey, without any friends having 4000-footer climbing experience, there was nowhere else to turn. Don't judge.

Figuring that shorter meant easier, I pulled the list from Peakbagger and sorted it by elevation to reveal the three shortest peaks: Whiteface, Tecumseh, and Isolation, all barely qualifying for the 4000-footer list, with respective heights of 4000', 4003', and 4003'. (Whiteface was incorrectly noted at 4000' in 2016. Alternate surveys established its height at 4020', which would have replaced it with Waumbek in the bottom three.) Tecumseh, which is essentially Waterville Valley Ski Resort, appeared reasonable enough, taking only 5.2 miles to get up and down. But I was still annoyed about not getting to ski Moosilauke and had already reserved Tecumseh for a climb-up/ski-down adventure. I also felt that I needed a little more experience under my belt before I was ready for that, so Tecumseh was out.

Isolation and Whiteface didn't appear to be good alternatives either. Isolation looked like a twelve-mile corkscrew of misery that I wasn't prepared to take on yet, and Whiteface only looked marginally better, requiring eleven miles of hiking into the unknown. These would not do. Scouring the World Wide Web for better options, I employed my razor-sharp detective skills and googled "easy 4000-footers in winter." Quickly, I hit pay dirt.

There were gobs of sites out there offering advice on climbing the 4000-footers, however, most of them were geared towards summer climbing. The ones that did touch upon winter hiking were mostly blogs cataloging someone's adventures in the Whites, providing some details about what to expect, but not enough to indicate the skill level required to base any decisions on. Nevertheless, after a few more clicks and some deft scrolls of the mouse wheel, I found Newenglandwaterfalls.com, with a page fully dedicated to climbing the 4000-footers in the winter. *Cue the choir—hallelujah!*

This site had exactly what I was looking for. It listed every mountain and provided difficulty ratings for climbing each of them during the winter months. It was perfect and I decided to use its ranking system as my marching orders. The level of difficulty was set on a scale of 1-10, where ten was the most difficult. Nothing had a rating of four or below, but one mountain had a rating of five: Mount Tom. Better yet, the website indicated Tom was easy for the winter beginner. *This is my guy.* Before making any more rash decisions though, I reviewed the entire list. Tecumseh looked even more promising now, with a rating of six. Definitely one of the easiest. There were a few others on the lower end of the scale, but Tom was clearly the best choice. For reference, I decided to check out the Osceolas—they were both nines! *Okay!* This was good. If I could tackle a nine without spikes, surely, I could tackle a nine or ten with spikes. *But first, let's make sure I can do a five.*

The first week of January was proving to be a quiet one workwise, so with nothing on the calendar for Wednesday, I left at dawn for Crawford Notch. Even with clear directions to the Avalon Trail and the Crawford Notch Depot, I blew right past the trailhead and had to drive around for ten minutes before I finally found where the trail left the road. The forecast called for high winds, but at the moment the sky was clear and the air was cool, with only a mild breeze; excellent conditions for the way my body overheats.

Even though I was finally equipped with spikes, I brought the Yaktrax for safe measure, figuring that the Yaktrax were better for thin ice while the spikes could be reserved for the thick stuff. *Smart, Matt. I know, I know.* Walking on rocks with microspikes is bad for their teeth, and causes them to dull and lose their traction, so it was good to have the Yaktrax on hand for when the terrain was a mix of rock and ice. I also wanted to make sure I had some backup in case the spikes broke. See? I was learning. The great thing about making mistakes is that you are always less likely to make them again, operative word being "likely."

I started out half walking, half jogging up the trail, doing what I like to call "wogging." With wogging, I don't overexert myself too soon, but keep the pace up so that I don't spend too much time on the lower sections of a long climb. It looks a little ridiculous as my backpack rattles around like a battered piñata, but it gets the job done.

At the first sign of ice, I dipped into my arsenal and pulled out the Yaktrax; there was still a lot of rock showing on the trail and I didn't want to risk wrecking the spikes. Not until I needed to anyway. I also assumed the spikes would be less comfortable on my feet and there was no point in being sorer than I had to be. The Yaktrax worked well and gave me the extra little bit of traction I needed.

Having the right equipment at my fingertips was liberating. Walking beneath the snow-capped trees, my mind free to turn its attention to the world around me, I had the sense that this was, finally, how my journey was supposed to be. The crisp, quiet air jarred dormant senses and thoughts awake. I could feel my toes and my fingers and the muscles in my back that had been idle for too long. I could hear the crackling and scraping of tree branches in the subtle zephyr. The air furled around me like a cold blanket and with each step I felt more connected to the ground beneath me, my soul tethered to the trees lining the trail. I thought about bears and coyotes, hoping and not hoping to see them. I thought about work responsibilities and how little they seemed to matter out here. I thought about having a bottle of wine with Liz at the Common Man.

Along the trail I bumped into a young couple on their descent. The man wore a beard and a red and black farmer's flannel. I tried to discern if he was a hipster from Boston trying to impress a girl, or a guy really trying to live the outdoor life up here in New Hampshire. He warned me it was windy at the top and that windier conditions were expected in the forecast, but all was fine below the treeline. Feeling hearty, I didn't worry too much about it. Tom was the only peak I was grabbing today, so if it was brutal at the summit, I'd simply make a quick getaway. As I said goodbye and turned to continue the ascent, he cheerily shouted "enjoy," which is the trail hiker equivalent of the boater's wave. I decided he was real. Plus, who else would be out here on a Wednesday in the middle of the winter?

At the spur trail leading to the summit, I came upon the only other hiker I saw that day: a slender man in his early fifties who had stopped to have a snack and enjoy the quiet. He was on his way down after summiting Field and said that he had considered Tom, but the "fierce winds" on Field convinced him to "leave Tom alone today." Besides, he continued, he had "done Tom plenty of times." As he stooped over his pack, fidgeting with its contents, he somehow looked out of place in this world. Like someone who kept getting laid off and didn't understand why. It was also clear that my presence wasn't welcome. Respecting his need for solitude, I skipped my snack and took off running up the spur trail, thrilled at the prospect of completing another mountain so soon after Osceola. Flying up the last 170 vertical feet it occurred to me—this was going to be my first ascent without any issues.

After all the warnings about heavy winds, I found the summit to have very little wind at all. My arrival was perfectly timed, and I caught a break in the gusts for a rest in the calm. According to my new winter hiking website, the views from Mt. Tom were considered "Fair," and I could see the argument for that, because there was a lot of tree cover at the summit blocking most of the views. But I was able to find a spot where I could sit and have my lunch looking out at Mount Washington and the Presidentials. It was majestic. I had the summit all to myself and was doing something that nobody knew about and few would consider. My body wasn't stiff or cold or sore; it was happy. Enjoying my PB&J reward, I studied the lines of the Presidential Traverse, edged by the sharp blue sky. I sighed and felt my mind expunged of all thought, want, or need.

Two gray jays rudely interrupted my summit reverie. They marched right up to my feet and inspected me, their black eyes penetrating my hands to see what goodies I possessed. They were oddly intrusive. Growing up, I always heard that blue jays were the bullies of the small bird world, knocking helpless little finches and chickadees off backyard feeders across America. *Were gray jays like blue jays? Only . . . with people?*

One little vulture hopped up past my outstretched knee, cocked his head and said, "drop the food, bub." Well, that's what his eyes said, I swear. As a peace offering, I threw a hunk of granola his way and watched him try to break it apart. First, he poked at it to see if he could whittle off a piece. Then he lifted it and dropped it several times on the ground to see if it would break on impact, but nothing was doing. Finally, his patience wearing thin, he opted to grab the whole bar in his beak and walk out of sight with it. "Greedy bugger, aren't you?" I said. The other jay looked at me now as if to say, "What about me?" I broke off another piece for him and we all enjoyed our lunch together. It was 10:45.

On the descent I was ecstatic. The weather had been magnificent, I had successfully claimed another mountain, and it was starting to feel like with every step along the trail I was making these mountains *mine*. A ridiculous notion, to be sure. The same mountain that can lift your spirits up one day, can chew you up and spit you out the next. If you don't respect the mountain, it won't respect you, and injuries and deaths may result. After all, climbing is not a symbiotic relationship: you are the servant, the mountain is the master. But on this day, I felt like the master, and however untrue that feeling is, it's one of the reasons we go up.

Chapter 6

Want-To-Be

My buddy Jonathan once described me as a diesel engine. He didn't mean I was slow and fat, although now that I think of it, maybe he did... *bastard!* Well, what I chose to believe at the time was that he was commenting on how I always seem to start climbs at a slow pace, but then pick up speed and climb with everlasting energy. Some people would resent the description, wishing they were more Ferrari than antiquated locomotive, but I loved it. After all, Ferraris end up crashing and burning from driving too fast, while diesels keep going and going and going. *Can't stop the diesel baby! Woot-woot!*

The diesel was gathering momentum. I hadn't had the proper focus with my initial climbs, but now that I was going, I was gaining energy and looking to knock off as many peaks as possible. Days passed too quickly after

Tom, and I was getting desperate to get back out there and grab another peak. After nine days, luck was on my side again, and I found a window in the schedule. Getting up at 4am was easy this time because I wanted to do this more than anything else I could imagine.

My new favorite website said Waumbek was the next easiest winter hike, and the views were supposed to be better than Tom's. I needed to look no further to make my decision. Gaining confidence from my experiences to date, I set out for Waumbek with no thoughts of failure, nor concern about the coldness of the air. I thought of the physical challenge and the sweat and the trudging and the beauty and the line of steam coming from my breath, and I accelerated towards all of it.

Recent snowfall called for snowshoes only a quarter mile up the trail, and I reluctantly strapped them on. I love snowshoeing while not being crazy about snowshoes themselves. Snowshoe steps are awkward and slow, and unless the snow is uniformly deep, you often trip on roots or rocks. But wearing them also makes you feel capable of conquering any terrain imaginable. An hour into my hike, listening to the packing of snow under my feet, my mind started to wander and I felt the explorer in me reawakened. *I want to see everything.* The snowshoes made it feel possible.

To climb Mount Waumbek, you need to climb Starr King first, which is on New Hampshire's "52 with a view" peak list. The "52" is a set of smaller peaks that offer spectacular views without putting you through the trials of gaining four thousand vertical feet to earn your reward. Seems like a good list, as the view from the top of Starr

King was hypnotic. Before me, a penetrating glow emanated from a crack in the horizon, where the all-encompassing cloud cover, smooth and unbroken, finally lifted enough to let light fill the firmament. Mountains loomed in the distance, obscured but present, while in the foreground sat the remains of a fireplace and a portion of its chimney—all that's left of a cabin that used to stand there. It looked like something Frodo Baggins may have come across on his way to Mordor, and it comforted me to know that should I get stranded there, I had a good place to make a fire with the matches I didn't bring.

Peak to peak, the stretch from Starr King to Waumbek is only about a mile, and I covered the distance by 9:45am. *Hey, I'm getting faster at this.* Finding a fallen tree to sit on, I dove into my usual morning meal, not sure what to call it because it was a little too early for "elevensies" and too late for breakfast. *Oh right, I guess you could call it brunch.* But I always associate brunch with mimosas and gossip, none of which were present here. Ever the wordsmith, I combined morning and lunch to create the only term I deemed appropriate for the meal: munch. Hey, sometimes the mountains draw deep thoughts out of you, and sometimes they don't.

But once I was situated, pondering the surrounding beauty, the nonsensical dissipated from my mind. In the distance, clouds remustered their strength, enveloping faraway mountains like time does stories. Unexpectedly silent and quick, their drastic action heightened my awareness of my proximate surroundings. Everything was so quiet. I stopped munching and listened intently, trying to detect a sound of any kind. I had never heard it so silent anywhere in my life. Everything—the air, the trees, the snow—was absolutely still. Time stopped. Like when you're a kid playing hide-and-seek, hiding behind your mother's clothes in the closet; the only sound you hear is your own breathing, which you try to quaff so you don't get found. I held my breath, even though there was no one around to find me. I can honestly remember that moment, savoring the sharp cool air and the stillness, more vividly than most of my other experiences in the mountains. I imagine I will for the rest of my life.

We were celebrating my daughter's third birthday that night, and I had taken the day off to get another climb in before enjoying the party. I still had plenty of time to get home, but sitting too long in the cold stiffens my body and gives me "seat-lock," where my knees and lower back lock themselves into a sitting position and resist the stretch back to standing. I hate seat-lock. I always feel better on the move. Besides, it was getting too dang cold whether I was sitting or standing, and I had already found what I was looking for. I decided it was time to go.

Heading down, I came across a father-and-son group—four dads and their boys—out for a little Friday bonding. I was ready to get off the mountain and see my daughter, so I blew by them pretty quickly, but the sight of them made me excited about future hikes with my kids. *I hope they'll want to do this with me someday. I hope they'll love it.* The boys were all smiling and asking too many questions to answer, hurrying their legs to catch up and make eye contact with their fathers. I hoped those dads knew how lucky they were.

A little further down the trail, an athletic couple in their early sixties passed by and asked me if spikes were necessary. When I assured them that they wouldn't come across any ice today, they beamed and thanked me, their smiles holding the mark of two people fulfilling some longstanding dream. After a few more steps down the trail, I looked over my shoulder and watched the woman drape her arm around her guy and move in for a kiss. They seemed to be floating their way up the path; two young dreamers on a new adventure. Even though I was anxious to get going, my feet held me, and I paused for a few moments to appreciate them. Marvel at them, really.

With each new adventure, it became increasingly clear that I wasn't the only one dreaming of climbing big mountains. I was constantly surprised by the number of cars at the trailheads and the various people climbing on such cold winter days. Undoubtedly, most of them were women or men like me, going it alone, but there were tons of couples and families out there as well, both young and old. Not everyone looked like an athlete either, or even capable of summiting, but summit they would. When I began this quest, I was hoping to have a singularly unique experience out in the wild, but as I made friends along the trail, I found myself entering this little community of unflappable spirits on the hunt for something better, and began to cherish my run-ins with strangers as much as my summit chances.

Who were these people, heading up the trails? What stories led them here? I know the idea of climbing mountains, especially in winter, is too daunting or too silly for most, and they naturally pursue other interests. They find other mountains to climb. Or at least some other hobby that requires less of a time commitment. Okay, fine, maybe a lot of us don't want anything at all except for a good TV show and a beer after a long day's work, but I have to imagine that this gets old for pretty much everybody at some point. During the grind of regular life, we all have other things we'd rather be doing with our time, don't we? Other things we might want to be?

Maybe you want to be an actor or study oceanography or learn the piano. Maybe you want to travel the world. Maybe you want to collect rare stamps or achieve the world record for holding the most marshmallows in your mouth at one time. Well, as the great Anonymous once said, "Do it now or forever wish you had." However ridiculous or trivial something may seem to others, if you have something eating at your heart and mind, you have to find a way to examine that truth and pursue it, or you will automatically shortchange the limits to your happiness. If marshmallows are your dream though, please don't dedicate your life to it. Maybe work on that for a weekend, see if you're any good, and then give it a rest. Let's not be crazy here.

Of course, everyone has to deal with the real world, punching the clock, paying the bills, moving mountains at home. That's just a reality if you want to have a roof over your head and food to eat. But people like to divide the world into dreamers and realists, when in actuality we can all be both. Many, many times, I have denied myself from pursuing some personal dreams in the short term because there were more pressing needs at hand: getting a job, providing for a family, building what society calls a "good life." These practical pursuits you owe to yourself, and your family, because without sensible perseverance, you will be a hard person for others to depend on in the future. On the flipside, if you completely shut yourself off from pursuing what stokes the fires of your soul, you run the risk of becoming rancorous, closed off, and, down the road, an unreliable source of wisdom for your children, grandchildren, and community. Nobody likes a bitter grandpa.

I'd been denying myself for a little too long though, I was starting to realize. Over time I'd forgotten how to balance my dreams with "real life," and was beginning to see that in doing so, I was limiting my growth as an individual. Dreams are, after all, what get you from who you are to who you are going to be. Getting back on the trail to pursue one of my dreams was doing more than restoring some much-needed balance to my life; it was reminding me that there are so many things I want to do and be.

Some dreams have to do with my personal character, the feeling being that if there is only one thing that I can achieve in this life, let me be someone who others can look up to. Someone that people care to know because doing so makes them feel better about their own associations and life choices. I hope my kids can look back years from now and say, "Dad did right by us," and my friends can look back and be grateful that I was around to make the hard times a little easier and the normal times a bit more fun. I want to be someone that people can feel in their bones that if shit ever hits the fan, they can always, always, call Matt. That's who I want to be. But more than that, each week I want to improve upon the man I was the week before, and I don't see how I can accomplish that by living a life of routine.

I want my life to be different. I want a life less ordinary. I want to come home with mud on my face and blood on my knees, and stories to tell. I want to pack as much activity into this life because I want it to be a life worth noting. I admit it. I also want to be a poet, a writer, a musician, a carpenter, a teacher, a great husband, a great father, a ski patroller, a little league coach, the world's greatest benefactor, an astronaut, the developer of the next great app, a senior Olympian, and a famous explorer. I'm not kidding. All of this is one hundred percent true. I'm a huge want-to-be. Not a wannabe, a want-to-be. And I want way more than a regular life.

Not that "regular" life isn't one heck of an adventure. It's cliché, but the most exhilarating experiences I've ever had were watching the births of my four children. Nothing can prepare you for that feeling, and there is nothing I have experienced on any mountain, or anywhere else, that can bring you so close to God all at once. Each time I witnessed one of them entering the world, I felt my heart getting ripped out of my chest and tears flowing uncontrollably from my eyes. The immediate thought I had when my daughter Chloe was born was how completely expendable my life is, and how I would do anything to protect her. That if God required me to throw myself in front of a bus to save her, I would do so without blinking. And the same overwhelming feeling washed over me again when her twin brother Max came out three minutes later, Jake two years later, and Phoebe four years after that. That feeling was so powerful and awe-inspiring that the other aspects of regular life—work, insurance payments, taxes, cocktail parties, recycled small talk with people at your child's soccer games, and so on—are so humdrum and mind-numbing that my soul yearns for other experiences that can bring back a slice of that magic. When I am not ensconced in the magic of watching my children grow, my mind wanders to other adventures that can touch my spirit. My mind can wander quite a bit.

Becoming a father was a discovery of feelings that I didn't know were possible, and I want to continue to make new discoveries for the rest of my life, capitalizing on the fact that I am here in this time and place, with precious few minutes to spare. There is a part of me that wishes I could have been a Native American exploring the wild frontier, or Lewis and Clark, doing the same. Or Leif Erikson, whose name I gave as the middle name for my son Jake, sailing forth to destinations unknown, exploring the ocean blue. I can think of few things I'd rather be doing than challenging a storm and sailing into port with a broken mast, a bloody arm, and a big smile on my face. *What's with this guy and bleeding?* I want to feel alive. Tested. Not by man and his constructs, but by Mother Nature and her strength. I know what you're thinking: *This guy is sick.*

But in this great opportunity called life, how can we not want to explore everything it has to offer? The world is an endless possibility of new towns, cities, shows, harbors, peoples, and lands to drink in. I want to experience all of it. Feel connected to all of it. But more than anything, I want to see mountains again, Gandalf—mountains! Because mountains are where few people journey, and it's this lack of people that can make the earth feel new again. Discoverable again. Watching the sunrise over a mountain range, without any homes or people idling in the valley below, feels like watching the rebirth of the earth. Making fresh snow tracks on the trail reminds me that fresh starts are possible, and that the world is in fact born over and over again. With each step up the trail, I'm reborn a little as well, and while the feeling doesn't hold the same magic as watching my children's births, it's a very solid second place. This is why I want to be a mountain climber. Pulling away from the Waumbek trailhead parking lot, I was beginning to feel like one.

Chapter 7

Naked

I always have trouble sleeping the night before a climb. It's not the climb I'm nervous about, but that I'm going to sleep in and screw up the plan. The same thing happens to me when I have a morning flight to catch or a morning meeting in Massachusetts, and I need to wake up extra early to beat the traffic. I'm always afraid of oversleeping.

The night before climbing Cannon I laid in bed for six hours, asleep for three of them. The other three were spent wide awake, alternating looks at the ceiling and my alarm clock. I was hoping to sleep in until five, but at four o'clock I realized that there was no point in waiting any longer for the alarm to go off and got myself out of bed. The extra hour was actually nice to have; there was no need to scarf down my raisin bran, and it gave me the chance to triple-check that my spikes were in my pack. I'm never forgetting my spikes again. Ever. They now live in my truck all year long.

In the quiet of my home, pacing around in the dark while my family slept, I loved the feeling that I was the only one in the world that was awake. In my early years, I used to lie awake in bed, wondering if it was possible that no one on earth was up but me. Then after applying some logic, I'd wonder if maybe everybody in America could have been asleep at the same time at any point in the last fifty years. After several nights of concluding it was possible, I remembered hearing about the city that never sleeps, and wished New York would go away. Vegas too.

Stepping outside, greeted by a bracing cold, I found myself smiling. I'd come to relish these predawn hours when the stars were out and nobody else was on the road except a few early risers. Driving through Amherst Village I came across a speedy runner, covered head-to-toe in reflective gear, and wondered if this fellow warrior believed that if he improved his time, he would extend his life. As if every run added to his longevity bank, rather than mildly breaking down his body as he overextended himself. *Gosh, Matt, that's cynical and probably not even fair. The guy probably can't find any other time to get exercise.* I suppose. Whatever the adventure of our choosing is, it's all a trick of the brain to keep us humming and forgetting our fear of death anyway. *Geez Matt, that's cheerful!* Sorry, I'm just saying, "I get it." I was probably a little jealous that he got to do what he loved by simply stepping outside, whereas I had to drive over two hours to meet my needs.

Rolling along the highway, heading north to conquer the land of Hoth, I turned my attention towards my own hobby and started fantasizing about the prospect of being the first one to break trail. The freezing temperatures convinced me that there was no chance anyone else was thinking of climbing today. *No chance!* But when I arrived at the trailhead, it turned out that I was late to the party once again. I would have guessed being beat to the parking lot on a beautiful summer morn, but during the winter? I mean, *who are these people?* Some people are flat out crazy.

No matter, today was going to be great. During the first few climbs, I found myself obsessed with getting to the top and conquering the mountain quickly, mainly because I was pressed for time and needed to get back for work or something else at home. Having to rush made all of the peaks seem so big, so indomitable, that my thoughts immediately turned towards beating them down as fast as possible. This breakneck pace wasn't sustainable, and it also felt like I was cheating myself out of a little fun. Wasn't the point of all of this to stop and smell the flowers? Or as it were, the snow? So, for Cannon, I deliberately gave myself the day to enjoy it, unfettered by societal or familial demands.

Having a full day to climb, I became more enamored with the process than the summit. The climb was the reward now: the effort, the steps, the connection to the mountain, the sounds of the birds, the wind rustling the leaves hanging on for dear life, the squirrels dashing away from my trail-crunching. My enjoyment of such things came incidentally on my previous hikes—wonderful byproducts of my goal to summit. Now experiencing them was the goal, and summiting Cannon was to be the byproduct of having a wonderful climb.

Even though Cannon is one of the shortest 4000-footers, the way up provided expansive views of the surrounding terrain, and I felt that I was witnessing more than I did on my previous climbs. Perhaps my consciousness was increasing. The snow was getting significantly thicker in the Whites by late January, and Cannon proved to be the hardest climb yet. The calculated distance was a little over five miles, but the ascent was fairly vertical, and my legs were working hard over the heavy snowpack. In the early going my undersized quads cramped up, and my old back injury felt rubbed and raw; physical reminders that I had quite a long path to go. But my aches eventually dissipated under the shining blue sky. Passing under the protective branches of the spruces parachuting snow upon my head, my mind escaped me, and my body hurt no more.

Granting myself the day made a difference. Without any other agenda, Cannon got the attention it deserved, and it returned to me a feeling of calm that my previous climbs lacked. I didn't need to worry about getting down quickly or what would happen if the temperature suddenly dropped. The other climbs had taught me how to better prepare and limit mistakes in my planning. All I had to do was "be" and enjoy the beauty that surrounded me. And beautiful it was.

You should know that I write this book with mixed feelings. When I tell you about my love of these mountains,

I don't want to encourage any of you to come to New Hampshire with your cars and your noise and your whohoopers and gardookas, and start mucking up the place. Especially if you're from Massachusetts. I want the beauty and tranquility of these mountains to remain mine and mine alone. *It's all mine, ya hear?* But my life is transitory, and it wouldn't do any good to keep my love a secret. Others should get to know the calm and inner peace these mountains bring. Everyone would be better off if they could find more time to walk the mountains.

That reminds me. There are some mountain snobs out there who argue that climbing to the top of a mountain, using only your feet, is plain old hiking, and not "true" climbing. You'll notice that I regularly use the terms hiking and climbing fairly interchangeably. I've done technical climbs and I've walked miles and miles. To me, if you are going up, you're climbing. Maybe it takes four limbs, maybe two, but either way you are pushing yourself upwards and that effort deserves a larger term than hiking. So, if you run into any dirtbags who call your peakbagging effort a simple walk, don't take their guff. You're a helluva something lugging your ass up a mountain of any kind, and you can smack them in the head with their carabiners for me. Okay, back to Cannon.

Even though the Kinsman Ridge Trail is only two miles in length, it took me a few hours to climb it. Sure, the heavy snows made for a long trudge, but some days simply go slower than expected. Neither exhaustion nor injury came into play. Maybe without any external demands for my presence I was subconsciously taking more time. I don't know. Whatever the cause, I was happy. The brilliant contrast of the snow against the aqua colored sky could make the grumpiest of souls dance a jig.

Nearing the summit, I fell into what was becoming a familiar habit of belting out songs off the top of my head. Above the treeline, "Mannish Boy" emerged from the vaults, and catching the last touch of blue sky I looked down over the valley and sang, "I'm a man. I'm a full-grown man. I'm a MAAAAN! I'm a rollin' stone." Then Clapton jumped into my head, probably because of his long association with the blues. I didn't want Clapton there so I quick-marched the rest of the way to the summit, hoping that would tire him out. Clapton's okay, but when it comes to the blues, B.B. King and him are so overplayed. The blues needs some new ambassadors.

Fortunately, Clapton didn't have the stamina to make it to the top and left me to enjoy Cannon's views in peace, which are absolutely magnificent in the winter. If you've ever gone skiing there, you'll know what I mean. From the summit vista, banded rivers of trees poured themselves over the edges of every subpeak, before rolling their way through the valley's troughs. The movement was mesmerizing and if it wasn't for the bitter cold, I would have had a difficult time peeling myself away. As the clouds blotted out the sun, I felt myself becoming lost to man, and realized I better get moving if I didn't want my body to get lost too.

One of the wonderful things about climbing is the changing perspectives. On the descent I noticed several trees that I had missed before on the way up. They were leaning towards each other over the trail, not close enough to touch, but close enough for their branches to form a row of frozen umbrellas that shielded me from the daylight. It didn't seem possible and so I stood there, frozen myself, pondering the ability of such large swaths of crystallized water to hang from the tiniest of lifelines. Craning my neck, mouth agape, I inched my way along until the developing clouds cast a deepening shadow over the trail. For a fleeting moment, I thought about Moosilauke and pending storms, but then considered the differences in my preparation and knew that there was nothing to fret about. The worst of my troubles would be a sunless descent.

After the frozen Gatorade debacle, I spent a lot of time researching ways to keep liquids from solidifying in below-freezing temperatures. Initially, what I found was a bunch of ridiculously expensive water bottles online, ranging *upwards* from $100. But then I found a blogger who used his extra wool socks to insulate drinks, noting that "the old ways are the best ways." I tried this on Tom and Waumbek, and it worked like a charm. Now, on a much colder day on Cannon, the bottle-in-a-sock trick worked again, and I was drinking sweet moving fluid the whole time, alleviating any stress about falling temperatures. To this day, the woolen sock trick has had a one hundred percent success rate. Who knew? I never would have discovered it had it not been for googling "how to keep drinks from freezing during winter climbing."

By the time I returned to the base of Cannon I was drenched in sweat, despite the frigid temperatures, and desperately needed to change out of my wet clothes. Having seen no one on the trail all day, and my car being the only one left in the lot designated for hikers, I figured *what the hey*, and stripped off all of my clothes before giving it any thought. Only then did I begin my search for a proper change of clothes in the back seat of the truck. Why I didn't figure out what to wear before getting naked is beyond me, but I was quite comfortable standing there in below freezing temperatures, for all the world to see.

What is happening to me? A couple months ago, changing butt-naked outside would have been unfathomable, but now I found the idea of someone stumbling upon me to be quite humorous. Somewhere in the recesses of my brain I determined that if I was spotted and questioned about my situation, I would simply reply: "been climbing." Or I'd grunt. Either response seemed perfectly acceptable. I was either too tired or too free to care.

After climbing into some fresh clothes, I posted a few pictures on Instagram, my new side hobby, detailing the beauty of my hike and the benefits of extra woolly socks for your water bottles. The picture of my woolly sock got twenty-nine likes! Social media is insane. And quite addictive. But as frivolous as social media can be, I appreciated being able to keep visual track of my experience so that I could reflect in real-time before certain moments escaped my memory. I didn't need Instagram, though, to remember what I did in the parking lot.

Driving home, I started to reflect on the climb and realized that while Waumbek gave me my most beautiful climbing moment to date, overall, Cannon was the most beautiful climb so far. On Cannon I felt a belonging that I hadn't quite experienced before—like nothing else mattered except my breath and my feet and the need to move. That my body was working with the mountain instead of against it or in spite of it. That I was developing a friendship with it. There were times when it even felt like the mountain and I were talking to each other. *Could that be?*

But then worldly consciousness came rushing back, and I thought, *What the hell am I doing? This is crazy! You are getting up at four in the morning to do these and have forty-three more to go? What the hell are you doing? You were just standing in a parking lot in the middle of the winter, NAKED . . . and LIKED it!*

Chapter 8

Uncashed Checks

Every month I get paid by a dead man. This has been going on since October of 2014, when one of my former tenants passed away in his early forties from cancer. He had set up his rent payments for automatic delivery and never got the chance to stop the recurrence before he died. I've tried everything to get the payments to stop coming. I reached out to the widow but she never responded to my calls or letters. I spoke to the brother-in-law who said he would contact the bank to stop the payments, but that never happened. I called the bank, but they said they couldn't stop the payments unless the account holder requested it, so there you go. Unless the widow or the brother-in-law puts in the request to stop the payments, there's nothing I can do but receive them, void them, and throw them out. Over, and over, and over again.

The gentleman who passed away was friendly and I genuinely liked him. During chats we found out that we had a lot in common and shared a similar history and set of interests. We even went to the same grad school program, which he had completed two years before I started it. Not much older than me, I recognized myself in him, and while I didn't know him well, his passing rocked my world. *That could be me.* Now I receive a monthly reminder from him about the precious minutes.

When the check arrives, I often open it and set it on my desk mantel, sometimes with the intention of calling the bank or the brother-in-law again, and sometimes because I don't know why. Sometimes I shred the check right away and sometimes I let a stack of them pile up. Sometimes I forget about the stack altogether, until another one arrives. They used to make me very uncomfortable, haunting reminders that they were, but now I'm resigned to acknowledge them with a perturbed gratitude. Unless I want to be a jerk and deposit them, giving the poor widow a heart attack when she sees her account depleted (if she even knows this account exists), I'm stuck with them. One day I found myself mindlessly staring at one of the checks for a few minutes. I couldn't take my eyes off it as I turned it over in my hand and reread his name. When my mind finally started up again, I decided to climb the Hancocks the next day.

Even though the first couple miles of the Hancock Notch Trail have a nice easy grade to them, I still heated up like a lizard in the Arizona sun after fifteen minutes of hiking. The day was overcast and gloomy, but I didn't mind because I was back in my happy place, unshackled from any want but to climb. In better physical shape now, I made quick work of the first three miles, and was feeling great about my chances of knocking off both Hancock and South Hancock in one hike. It was looking like this would be my first successful two-summit day, and everything was going swimmingly until I started up the Hancock Loop Trail to ascend South Hancock.

South Hancock in winter is *hard*, and I couldn't have done it without microspikes. Slipping and tripping my way up the forty-five-degree pitched slope, I wondered if this time I wouldn't be thwarted by a lack of preparation, but a lack of ability. I also couldn't stop thinking about little Atticus. In between climbs I was reading up on other climbers' stories, particularly those who ventured into the White Mountains, and had recently read *Following Atticus*, which was about the author Tom Ryan and his intrepid little Scottish schnauzer taking on the forty-eight. Atticus was in a word, amazing. But before I say anything more about him, I should qualify my remarks by making this abundantly clear: I am not a big pet guy.

Our dog Boomer was pretty cool and all, and I liked him, generally speaking, but I didn't look at him and think "best friend." And I certainly didn't want to go hiking with him again. I tried it once and he made me chase him through the woods for three hours before I finally gave it up. After a couple more hours he came back home on his own; he wasn't lost at all, he was just messing with me, the big jerk. So, I didn't need the headache of yelling "Booooooomer" all over the White Mountains while trying to bag the forty-eight.

Boomer was trained too. He could sit, shake hands, stay, and wouldn't descend upon his dog bowl until you told him it was okay. When he was on the leash, he even heeled. Well, sometimes. But there was one command the little bastard decided was totally beneath him: come. Every time I said "Boomer, come," he gave me a "fuck you" look and then ran in the opposite direction. I respected his gumption, but hated his camaraderie. My buddy Matt used to email me funny stories about his dog, referring to her as "The World's Greatest." I'd share stories about "The World's Mangiest" in reply.

But I loved Atticus, who liked to climb mountains and lead his owner to the top of every peak. I loved how he would sit at the summits and look out at the view, as if in deep meditation, contemplating life beyond human understanding. He never seemed to whimper or falter, despite being so physically limited for the endeavor, and I found myself wishing more people were like him as I read about his adventures. But truthfully, I didn't give him or the book too much thought until I climbed the Hancocks in the wintertime. On South Hancock, I was in awe of Atticus.

Several times I needed to climb on all fours over the deep snow and buried ice, and I marveled at how fat (self-described) Tom Ryan, and his little dog with no microspikes on his feet, made it up this steep incline. The dog was a wonder. A little canine Napoleon, jumping through miles of snow that reached above his head, resilient in all kinds of weather. Mr. Ryan was also pretty admirable, and both of them reminded me that the climbing game depends more upon your mental toughness than your physical condition.

It was a Wednesday and apart from the spirits of Tom and Atticus, it was the first time I was utterly alone in the mountains. I didn't see a single soul all day. Not in the parking lot and not on the trail. Later it occurred to me, nobody would ever know how ridiculously hard this climb was, no matter how well I relayed it, and I decided that was okay. They didn't need to. That was simply the tradeoff for getting to do something like this on a day when no one else can.

My quest had a lot to do with tradeoffs, especially since I was trying to do all of the 4000-footers in one year. *How to do this so it doesn't infringe upon work, family and friendships? How do I scratch this itch so that I'm not unhappy?* My main strategy was to cram my workweek into four days because I didn't want to have climbing suck up any weekend time. Weekends were for my family and with four kids I didn't think it would be fair to Liz, after a long week of taking care of them, to ask her to add one more day at home without me. Fitting in the climbs during the workweek was the best option because she already slated the weekdays as "time without Matt." Besides, I've gone climbing on a Saturday before, and all that night Liz sounded like Marge Simpson, upset with Homer for making a drunken fool of himself in front of the whole town again. *Mmmmmmm.*

Being idle during work hours is not my forte, so I typically work like a monster on Monday and Tuesday, packing in ten to twelve hours with little break. This usually leaves Wednesday with a little lull, which I use to plan out the rest of the week, or lately, go for a climb. There are many weeks where I feel like Monday and Tuesday are quite sufficient to accomplish what others will do in five, only because I cannot relax my work pace. I'd rather get everything done so I can leave work early and go do something else. Life is a series of tradeoffs like that, where if you put in the extra time on one thing today you can go enjoy something else tomorrow. Same thought process goes into my career. I want to retire early, like at age fifty, so I rationalize that if I work twice as hard now, I can work half as hard later. I don't want to fully retire at age fifty, truly, but would like the last half of my life to "work" on only the things that I love; like climbing and writing.

The tradeoff of climbing the forty-eight in one year was that despite the exhaustion, it was worth it to prove to myself that I could do it. Not only for me, but for my family as well. In order for me to be a good father and someone my family could rely on, I felt that it was not only important to always be available to them, but to also know how to be self-reliant. Scratch that, SUPREMELY self-reliant. Heck, I wanted my kids to know that their dad is the nicest guy on the planet and a giver of great hugs, but if called upon, could kill all the other dads in Amherst with his bare hands. *What, too extreme?* Okay fine, that I could save all of the other dads' lives if necessary. And what better physical test of one's own self-reliance is there, without hurting any other dads, than mountain climbing?

But when I walk the trails alone, nobody is there to see if I am successful or feeling well or getting tired. Nobody sees when an old spine injury causes my back to lock up, or when my feet have so many blisters that I need to wrap them in duct tape in order to keep going. Sometimes I'm so tired I'm nauseous, and my knees are in such agony, all I want to do is sit down, but I can't sit down because there are so many more miles to go. Why put myself through it? Who cares?

The same can be asked when you are working late at night, trying to go the extra mile for that project or your boss or your career. Nobody sees you when you're working hard, and nobody knows the effort you put into something. Nobody is really aware of your heroics. You may trick yourself once or twice into thinking they are, but to sustain that level of commitment, you have to do it because it matters to you and you alone. Because you care. And if the work itself isn't enough to make you care, you need to find the reason why it's important for you to work, so that you can continue to propel yourself forward. That's the mental edge that allows people to climb big mountains, be good parents, and pursue their dreams.

There comes a point in every life when you recognize your unfulfilled dreams, and you have to take the chance to do something about it before it's too late. Because who knows what happens when all of this is done? Maybe you'll get reincarnated, maybe you'll go to Heaven, or God forbid, someplace else. Maybe nothing happens to us when we die. But the one truth you can count on is that you have one chance to live *this* life, regardless of what is true for you on the other side, so you better go out there and live it, and live it well. Make your tradeoffs so you not only do what you want, but live the way you want, and give of yourself to the people you love before the moment passes you by. Nobody wants an epitaph that reads "missed his chance." And at the end of the day, it doesn't matter if anybody ever knows the effort you put in to reach your dreams. You'll know, and knowing you gave it your best shot is the only measurement you need to record.

Edward Abbey once wrote in *Desert Solitaire* that death would be most welcome in the mountains. I'm paraphrasing, but he essentially asked: what could be better than finding yourself alone in the wilderness, a life well spent, exerted, and lying down there for a final rest? That rather than living a life of ease, dying comfortably of old age at your desk, you did everything you wanted to do, rose to face life's challenges, and had your mettle tested. That you lived and loved life. While not planning on dying in the mountains anytime soon, I can certainly subscribe to the theory that dying in pursuit of my dreams—living the life I want and giving it my best shot—whether or not anyone bears witness to it, is certainly preferable to dying tied to my desk. Especially my desk, where rest a dead man's checks.

Chapter 9

Not Golf

I used to have a theory that the entire demise of the male species in America could be traced back to men's singular interest in the game of golf. While adventure awaits, too many of us seem completely content to walk in circles around the same eighteen lawns, over and over again, fixated on trying to make par. To make par! You know what par means? AVERAGE! It means you are getting the ball in the hole the allotted number of tries you are *supposed* to do it in! I didn't get it.

But my son Max and his friend Matt have showed me that I had golf all wrong. It's been a great sport for them to meet up and spend a sunny day together, unencumbered by parents and supervision. They love it. And as for men, I suppose a large part of what makes golf so appealing is that it can be done mindlessly or with mindful improvement on the brain. Dealer choice. Men of different abilities can play together while having an activity where they can drink beers and smoke cigars without their wives judging them. And the wives are happy to let them go do it, because as long as the men are contained within an eighteen-hole limit, they can't get into too much trouble and embarrass themselves. Not to mention, golf is convenient, with courses a stone's throw away from every turnpike and byway you can imagine. Completely unlike your nearest mountain.

But when did watching Breaking Bad, cracking open another IPA, and planning the next round of golf become the pinnacle of our desires? I often hear men wish how they could do "something crazy" like climb a mountain, as if getting in the car and driving north to a trailhead was totally beyond the realm of conceivability. How could that be? Where have all the Edmund Hillarys gone? The Shackletons? The Fridtjof Nansens? There's nothing wrong with wanting to play golf now and then, but how do we figure out what life is all about by spending every weekend walking in loops, doing a hobby of convenience? Maybe some can, but I can't, so I head to the mountains, which helps clear my mind so that I can reestablish what my purpose is, and perhaps even reestablish myself as a good person. One who can better tolerate the game of golf, anyway.

Every trip up and down a mountain peak feels like Mother Nature is granting me a fresh start. The clean air and the wind whispering through the trees renew my spirit, reminding me that I don't need to get pulled down into the muck of civilization and society. That I can rise above it, and come down the mountain a better man, better able to exercise my ability to treat people better than they treat me. I also think that any time you're struggling with something, or you're depressed, the physical act of climbing a mountain can bring you back to a contemplative place where you can sort through your questions and find, if not the whole answer you are looking for, a little nugget of truth to build upon.

It was with all of these notions in mind that I set out to tackle the Tripyramids on my thirty-ninth birthday. Spurred on by the fact that I was beginning my fortieth year, I decided it was imperative to get another two-peak day behind me, and settled upon North and Middle Tripyramid as my targets. I needed to go without knowing exactly why.

At the summit of Middle Trip, I caught an incredible view of Waterville Valley, its ski trails basking in the only direct sunlight the early morning had to offer. Pausing for a few pictures, I set my phone upon a tree branch and turned on the timer function to take a posed "selfie" of myself looking out at Waterville Valley. Yeah, that's right, I took a selfie. Hey look, with nobody to climb with, I had to use myself as a model, and I wanted to remember the scale of the view. Okay?

Looking out at Waterville, my mind turned to skiing, and I was reminded of my failure on Moosilauke. I suppose Moosilauke will be synonymous with failure forevermore. What only seconds before was a marvelous and inspiring view, turned into a portrait of unfinished business. I'd be lying if I told you I didn't growl under my breath, just a little bit. There was no doubt what my next mountain would be, and how I would do it.

On Osceola I started using the voice recorder app on my smartphone to record observations from each climb, and I was loving the ability to take notes in real-time before they were lost forever. But on the Tripyramids my mind was completely empty and free, and I didn't bother recording anything at all. It was such a tranquil morning that I got lost in my footsteps early on, and the time passed quickly, allowing me to reach the top of Middle Trip in a little under three hours. Stumbling upon the summit before I was aware of its approach, I realized that my mind had been mostly blank for the entire ascent. In fact, I hardly remembered climbing at all.

What I do remember was sharing the trails with a few middle-aged guys, and I was comforted by the idea that they must be dealing with the same issues I was. But there was also this younger guy, fairly tall and muscular, wearing an "Army" hat. I have enormous respect for the military and am quite in awe of their sacrifice, but right from jump street, this gentleman was a little odd. The first time I saw him, he greeted me overenthusiastically, like I was his long-lost best friend. But later, when I bumped into him further up the trail, I said, "hello again," and a deeply uncomfortable minute passed as he stared at me without saying a word. It was like he had never seen me before in his life. Then, when I saw him a third time on my way down, he was friendly again, and excitedly told me about his idea to butt-slide Sabbaday Falls.

"I've heard people do it—I think I'm going to do it! You want to go?" he invited. I confessed I didn't know where they were and had never heard of anyone butt-sliding them. I asked him to point them out and he gestured towards an enormous cliff that dropped a thousand feet, at what looked like a ninety-degree angle. Covering the entire length of the cliff were two frozen waterfalls, and butt-sliding them would be impossible to survive. I looked at him to see if he was joking; his locked expression confirmed he wasn't. Spidey-senses kicking in told me that I shouldn't take my eyes off this guy, but then again, staring back at him for too long seemed like a good way to piss him off. I returned my gaze to the falls because I didn't know what else to do with my eyeballs.

I later learned these weren't the actual falls most people visit, but if that's what he thought looked like a good idea to slide, there was little doubt that this guy was off his rocker. In fact, his whole demeanor had me wondering if he had a death wish, and I couldn't shake the feeling he had a weapon on him. Rather than tell him that I would be absolutely terrified to join him wherever he was going, I told him I had other plans. He stared at me a little too long with one of those faraway prison stares you hear about, and I concluded it was time to get away.

A part of me felt bad because I knew about some ex-military taking to the trails to manage their PTSD, and I wondered if that was what was going on with this guy. But I was also concerned for my safety. I wished him good luck and turned to go. He was the only person that ever made me feel uncomfortable my entire time in the mountains.

As I took my leave, another climber reached the summit, and Army man immediately tried to recruit him for the falls. The new guy was intrigued and listened to the pitch. Not feeling entirely good about leaving this hiker alone with Army man, I interjected that without an ice axe or a helmet, it looked too dangerous for me (emphasizing the "me" part so as not to insult Army man), and then quickly went on my merry way. Heading down the trail, it finally occurred to me that Army man didn't have a helmet or an ice axe either. *Holy shit, he'll die if he does do it*, I thought. Maybe he really did have a death wish. And then I thought of Edward Abbey noting that if you're going to die, why not let it be in the mountains.

The rest of the descent was pretty fast, which is par for the course. I'm not a big guy, maybe 180 pounds, give or take a few, but on mountain descents I lumber like I'm six-foot-eight, 280, especially when I'm running away from guys with death wishes. I know I said men could stand to be a little more adventurous these days, but that doesn't mean when the hairs on the back of your neck stand on end, you can't run like your pants are on fire. Running scared maybe wasn't the memory I was shooting for when I headed out the door that morning, but hey, at least it wasn't golf. I can't recall a single round of golf I've played. I can remember the time I threw out a disc in my neck on the driving range, or the time I accidentally hit both of my parents with a golf ball from two consecutive shots with my pitching wedge, but a clean round of golf? I have no recollection of that.

Chapter 10

Chasing Tecumseh

I didn't want to get up this early. Not. At. All. I wasn't tired but I didn't feel like going outside in the cold and leaving the warmth of my bed. I wanted to say good morning to Liz and the kids. I wanted to go back to normal life. Everything in my body said, "Stay in bed man. Come on dude, let's sleep." Only the tiny mind-light of my conscience insisted I get up. It chastised me, saying "Come on, you started this thing and you're not even halfway done. GET. MOVING." With half a heart, I rotated my feet off the bed, stood up, and went to the closet to get dressed. Stupid conscience.

My conscience was right though. Days are days. You can't wait for better ones, or warmer ones. When you set a day for a plan you made, it's set, and you just have to do it.

Unless it's dangerous, of course. But if you let one day slide, it only gets easier to skip the next one, and then the next one, and before you know it a heap load of time has passed and you are nowhere closer to reaching your goal. Besides, the worst part of waking up so early is the first minute. Every minute that follows gets progressively better. Once you are driving down the highway and you see the beautiful sunrise, and you know where you are heading, you can't believe the "old you" wanted to stay in bed an hour ago. That guy misses out on so much.

I live in a very old house with large pine-board flooring, which makes sneaking out almost impossible (take note, kids!). But I somehow managed to creak my way down the second-floor hallway, down the front stairs, and into the kitchen, all without disturbing anyone except the chipmunks residing in the basement. And the dog. But not much. Boomer lifted his head, rolled his eyes, and went back to bed. The floors are our only protection from burglars. Not wanting to wake anyone else, I hastily ate some Honey Nut Cheerios and creaked out the side door, back towards my truck and the great northern highway.

This next climb was going to be my tenth summit, and I decided to make it special by doing what I couldn't do on Moosilauke. *I know, I know. Issues.* But I hated the idea of setting my mind on something and not being able to accomplish it. As much as I recognized leaving Grand Teton was the right thing to do, it still bothers me I didn't get it done. It's a real problem I have. Unsuccessful summits taunt me, teasing me that there's something I wasn't strong enough to do. And if anything or anyone tells me there's something I can't do, well, *oh! Ooooohhhhh!! Grrrrrrrrr.*

In the previous weeks, I'd been researching the three commercial ski mountains on the 4000-footer list: Cannon, Wildcat, and Tecumseh (aka Waterville Valley). Figuring one of these to be my best bet for a climb-up/ski-down experience, I scoured the blogs and message boards for advice on which one to choose. Most of what I found, though, were gobs of internet trolls, ripping into people like me for even considering this. And they really ripped into those wanting to carry their skis instead of "skinning" up.

In case you don't know, there are two main ways to climb up and ski down a mountain. You can either "skin up," where you attach sticky carpets to your skis, enabling you to hike up the hill with your skis on your feet, or you can carry your skis on your back like a boss. In the backcountry world, people tend to think you are an idiot if you choose the latter option. Without owning any skins, I was planning on being an idiot once more.

But I couldn't believe how many jerks were out there, questioning people for wanting to skin up a commercial ski mountain, when there are so many more beautiful places to do "real" backcountry skiing. To an extent, I agreed with these pontificating purists, but really? What if you are a total noob? To the haters I say: if you were half as cool as you think you are, you wouldn't try to swell your egos by criticizing the whims and wills of others. If you are new to the sport, are you really going to venture off alone into backcountry areas you know nothing about? Everyone has to start somewhere. I always like seeing people skinning up commercial mountains; it's awesome to see people out there who actually want to try such things. Noobs are badasses too, people!

Cannon's website, however, didn't indicate noobs were welcome, even if you paid to play. I also found reports of Cannon employees yelling at people for climbing up the hiking trail with skis on their backs. That didn't sound fun. Getting yelled at would seriously dampen the mountain stoke, ya know? So, Cannon was out. Wildcat, on the other hand, welcomed skinners, but you had to use a designated ski trail and pay ten bucks for the privilege. *Well, no thanks to that.* How am I supposed to enjoy my mountain reverie with downhillers flying past me every few minutes? I wanted peace and quiet, and to see as few mountain employees as possible. And I definitely didn't want to pay for it. Ten bucks isn't a big deal, but it's the principle of the thing. If I'm using my own power to get up the mountain, I'll give myself the ten bucks, thank you very much. Plus, there was the fact I wouldn't be skinning. Would Wildcat even allow me to walk up the ski trail with skis on my back?

So, I pinned all of my hopes on Tecumseh and looked to Google images for a sign. When I finally found some pictures of a few guys carrying skis up the Tecumseh hiking trail, I moved to the edge of my seat. *This looks promising.* Better still, I couldn't find any reports of anyone getting yelled at. *Good, good.* One guy actually noted that some Waterville employees were pleased to see him carrying his skis up. *Yahtzee!* This was it; Tecumseh, or Waterville Valley, or whatever you want to call it, was the one.

At Waterville's base, I couldn't locate the trailhead, so I ran up to the lodge for a look-see. It was the 7th of March, a Monday, which I planned on purpose, figuring the mountain would be pretty empty as most people were focused on starting the workweek. I also figured the ski bums would be a little foggy after working and partying all weekend, so if I could get on the trail before the lifts opened, I'd avoid detection. Looked like I was right; the place was a ghost town. After a pit stop inside the lodge, I circled around the parking lot a few times until I found a little sign marking the Tecumseh hiking trail. Parking as close to the trailhead as I could, I hurriedly grabbed my gear and gave one last look around to make sure the coast was clear before disappearing into the woods.

Wogging the first three hundred yards to ensure further concealment, I was feeling the extra weight of the skis, and perhaps, expectations. Typically, I ate an apple about a mile into each hike, the natural sugars giving me a little pep I sorely needed, but I wasn't going to make it that far today without any nourishment. I hit the brakes, and propping myself up against a tree, crushed my first apple of the day.

Sweaty but revived, I took a moment to look around and noticed it was snowing. *It's actually snowing!* What are the chances? On the day I chose to use skis, it was actually snowing! Deep within my blood I could feel the call of a thousand Viking warriors shout, "to Valhalla!" and I spontaneously sprouted a two-foot beard. Oh, this was going to be a good day.

Whether it was my desire to be a Viking, the need to do something others can't, or my subconscious railing against the internet trolls who bemoan backcountry skiing on commercial mountains, I flew up Tecumseh, reaching the top in only two hours. *That felt so easy. I must be getting in good shape.* Resting my pack against a scraggly pine at the summit, I couldn't help but admire it. Something about it, laden with ski equipment and extra gear, looked more real than it did when I set out from the parking lot. The pack was no longer what I wanted it to be. It was. It had actually been used to do what it was intended for and looking at it gave me satisfaction.

Now it was time to ski. From Tecumseh's summit you have to traverse across the Sosman Trail to get over to the groomed ski trails of Waterville Valley, and I couldn't hustle fast enough. After a few minutes I popped out on a little hillside, fifteen feet above the terminus of the High Country Ski Lift, where two early bird skiers were getting off the chair. I watched as they passed below me, idly talking, completely unaware of my presence. *They didn't see me.* A tickle of pride swelled inside me—it felt like I had just robbed secret treasure from the vaults of Fort Knox. *Nobody knows I'm here!*

Because of the markedly warmer weather, I had no trouble putting on my ski boots this time, and within minutes I was sailing ribbons of white ocean, clear of humanity. To avoid any possibility of being spotted and getting reprimanded for skiing without a lift ticket, I skied away from the center of the mountain and all of its potential encumbrances. Skis off my back and on my feet, my body felt lifted and light as I sped down trails named "Tippecanoe," "Lower Tippy," and lastly, "Lower

Periphery." Out of my periphery I could see the base of the mountain was devoid of life, and when the trail came to an end, I swiftly unbuckled my skis and marched off to my car, mission complete.

You may think I was being overly paranoid about getting caught, and the irony is not lost on me that I'm now writing about it, fully confessing my crimes. If a representative of Waterville Valley reads this, I will gladly pay the fine if there was one to pay. I knew of no fee, but I didn't want to hang around and find out if there was one either. The day was too perfect, and all the more exciting that nobody was even aware I was there. I didn't want anything or anybody to spoil it.

There's something about climbing alone that makes you feel so powerful, yet humble. Like with each step upwards, you are somehow pulling these two emotions together, and yourself closer to center as a result. For me, it was becoming customary to hit a Zen-like state about an hour into each climb, where my body felt totally relaxed and my mind cleared of all worry. After another hour I usually hit a euphoria state, where I'd either start singing a song, or as I did on Tecumseh, be overcome with the feeling that I am lucky to be alive. Lucky to be here and that I have been given some great gift. What a gift it is to be out in the world, with sound body and mind, pulling mountain air into my lungs.

Tom Ryan, of *Following Atticus* fame, wrote that when he got to the top of a mountain, he often liked to say a prayer for someone. When I first read that, I thought it sounded a little too self-serving, like he was trying to get the reader to think he was a great guy or something. But I was wrong to feel that way. At each mountain summit, you feel stronger than you did before, and grateful, which makes you feel like giving something back to people, even something as small as a prayer.

As forty approached, it suddenly seemed that friends and family were starting to suffer more, and I occasionally found myself praying for them. I prayed a lot for my son's friend, who was diagnosed with cancer when he was only seven, and I asked God why I should be so fortunate to have four healthy children, while his parents have to face losing their only one. This would then make me nervous about bringing my own good fortune to God's attention, so I'd pray twice as hard for Liz and the kids, which inevitably made me feel guilty for being so selfish. But I couldn't help it; all of my fears are wrapped up in them. I pray to God to keep them safe and help me be strong for them.

Trying to be a good man, a strong man for others to depend on, is a complicated process. We don't naturally communicate our feelings as well as women, and we don't want God to solve our problems for us. We want to be the ones to handle everything for our people. To be the ones who can take care of it all. Battling the elements, climbing all of these mountains, lugging skis upon my back, certainly had something to do with showing that. But I'm also not a "tough guy," hiding what I'm feeling (the evidence being in your hands). I don't want to go through life leaving things unsaid. As Bill Burr says, being a tough guy is a brutal existence, where you've "got to hold on to all of that shit, slowly dying inside." That doesn't sound good.

When I was young, I thought what society wanted from me was to be tough, but acting tough is not the same as being unafraid. In fact, many times it's the wall we put up because we are afraid. Being unafraid means being willing to share exactly how you feel about something—to always tell the truth, without fear of judgment. This doesn't mean speaking rudely or without empathy, but it doesn't do anybody any good to let your feelings go undisclosed, and it can only hurt you to bury them. Being unafraid is always being true to yourself. In this regard, I still wasn't quite the man I wanted to be.

My whole life, I wanted to be a writer, and I spent too much time being afraid to climb that particular mountain. The more I climbed, the more I started to ask myself: How can I look my kids in the eyes and tell them to pursue their dreams if I never do it myself? How can I be of full service to anybody when I short-change myself? Forty was prompting me to look at all of the mountains I had been avoiding, so that mine would never be a life of regret. As Chief Tecumseh said, "When it comes your time to die, be not like those whose lives are filled with the fear of death, so that when their time comes they weep and pray for a little more time to live their lives over again in a different way. Sing your death song and die like a hero going home." When I read those words it occurred to me, this is the only way I want to live. So, I started writing. Really started writing.

Chapter 11

Kinsmen

The stress of everyday life was weighing on me: the crook who stopped paying his rent and then counter-sued me in a retaliation effort to prolong his eviction, the flat tire forming on my truck in the parking lot, the lack of time I had to get to all of the things I needed to get to this week. But the icy trails demanded my attention and my stress dissipated with the mountain breeze. Within minutes I felt very far away from everything down below.

Ten mountains ago I would have said, *you fool, you can't go climbing at the start of a workweek—not with everything you've got going on!* But I was starting to get the hang of balancing my new endeavor with work life. Actually, a lot of my work can be done on the mountain these days. Now that our smartphones are like minicomputers, you can reply to an email from a mountaintop or the beach, and nobody will get wise to your actual whereabouts unless you write it down in a book. From my phone I can sign contracts, log work orders, and address accounting issues. Oftentimes I'm required to listen to people complain, so why not do that while doing something good for me? Most people don't even want to talk on the phone anymore and prefer to correspond via email or text, making it all the easier to engage with clients in a professional manner.

Today I was climbing North and South Kinsman via the Lonesome Lake Trail. The lake was still frozen, and I considered crossing it, having done it years ago with Liz and some friends, but that was in the thick of winter. This was March and the melting ice didn't give me the warm and fuzzies. If there was a guinea pig walking across, that would be something, but the only company I could find were the birches crinkling in the beating wind. The risk was too great, so I decided to go the long way. It was a good thing too because when I reached the other side of the lake, much of the ice was receding, leaving ten feet of exposed water along the shoreline. I would have never made it. *Who's a smart guy? Who's a smart guy?!* I wanted to pat my own head. Passing the Lonesome Lake hut, I heard a couple of voices from within—the only signs of human life—and started up the Fishin' Jimmy trail.

The trail wasn't easy. Spikes weren't enough to keep from slipping on the steeps, and I was constantly grabbing for spindly trees to catch my balance. I found myself looking forward to summer hiking for the first time. Halfway to the summit I came upon a field of toppled ash trees, providing an unfettered view of the valley below. But instead of the view, I couldn't take my eyes off those trees. They were all blown back in the same direction, their branches hacked off. A sea of dead soldiers, mowed down by enemy bullets. I had heard of "microbursts" before, where sudden blasts of 100mph winds can downdraft onto a mountain during a thunderstorm, and I wondered if this was in fact the grisly scene of a multiple herbicide. Heavy winds answered me, knocking me back a couple steps.

To get to South Kinsman you have to hike over North Kinsman first, and then climb back over North Kinsman yet again on your way out, so you actually end up summiting three mountain peaks in one day, albeit one of them is a repeat. This happens a lot with the 4000-footers. Whenever I end up having to climb back over a mountain I already did, I often think about the people trying to accomplish what is known as "the grid." This is when people who are really sick—like way, way sicker than me—feel the need to climb all 4000-footers once in *every month of the year*. This doesn't mean they do it all in one year, but that at some point in their lives they will have climbed all forty-eight mountains during the month of March, and also in April, and in May, and so on. In other words, they will have completed, at a bare minimum, 576 ascents of the same flipping mountains, over, and over, and over again. Like I said, sick.

But I'm not without empathy for these extremists, and while passing over North Kinsman I thought that if I were a gridder, I would climb these peaks on, say, June 30th, and then spend the night camped somewhere below South

Kinsman. Then, on July 1st, I'd go in the reverse direction so that I could claim two months for two mountains in the shortest amount of time possible. But maybe the gridders don't care about efficiency. What do you suppose they are running from, anyway? To spend that much time in the mountains, they must be running away from something, right? Are they battling demons? Or are they the healthiest, sanest people on the planet? How much climbing is healthy? What makes someone choose to climb the same mountains again and again?

Everything in life can be broken down into a climbing choice. To climb or not to climb, that is the question. From the executive trying to take his company public, to the nun behind closed doors of a monastery trying to connect with God, to the teacher trying to elevate her students, to the man searching for independence in the mountains—all of it is an effort to be something you want to be, to do something you want to do, and to live a life that you think is more fulfilling than what others have chosen. Even the layabouts, looking to veg out and suck the marrow out of life, have made a choice that they think is better than what others have chosen: the choice not to climb. *Just chill, man, let the mountain be*, they say. Some choices are misguided and lazy, but they are choices nonetheless. The choice to give up is an active mental effort, whether you believe people can help it or not.

These gridders though, I don't know. I guess it's the equivalent of someone who really loves their job, finding each day interesting, even if the experiences from one day to the next overlap. But why not climb some different mountains? Or have some different experiences, for Pete's sake? After all, this isn't a job, and if your feet are free to take you wherever you choose, there are 1,000,761 *other* mountains in the world to do besides the 4000-footers of New Hampshire. I can't help but feel like the gridder's life balance is a little out of whack. Like the workaholic that never spends time with their kids. No, climbing the same mountains over and over again is not for me. Why limit our experiences such? I'd like to keep having new experiences before it's too late to have them.

Several months earlier, my grandfather, with whom I was close, passed away. At the funeral, a friend in his sixties told me how excited he was to retire so that he could randomly call up a buddy and finally go on a weekend ski trip to Utah. As he spoke, all I kept thinking was, *but what if your buddies are now too tired to go? Or worse, what if they die soon?* Morbid, I know, but realistic. I decided I couldn't wait that long; my buddies and I booked a ski trip to Utah a few weeks after the funeral.

Time is, after all, a precious commodity, a lesson I absorbed early in life from my dad. When he was a young boy, he lost his oldest brother to cystic fibrosis. Then he lost his mother to Alzheimer's when he was barely in his twenties. I think the way he responded to these early losses, and to ensure he didn't live a life of regret, was to move through life at breakneck speed. I have never met a sharper, more complex man, and keeping up with him has been one of the great challenges of my life. Like all people, Dad sometimes uttered the phrase "life is short," but when he said it, you could sense he really meant it. It's always the belief in words that serves to motivate better than the words themselves.

But I needed to look no further than my own life to understand how precious time is. In childhood, I battled debilitating asthma that left me struggling to breathe throughout the day. No amount of medication fully stemmed the attacks, and there were many days when a Ventolin inhaler offered little relief. Nights were even worse, and I spent many of them standing in a steaming hot shower, trying to open my airways. Sometimes my parents would sit outside the bathroom door to make sure I was okay, but the attacks came more often than they ever knew. Many nights, when showers didn't do the trick, I would spend hours sitting up in bed, trying to keep my wheezing to a minimum so that it didn't wake them. The fight to breathe was so constant that I developed an odd habit of trying to pinch the skin away from my breastplate to see if I could relieve some of the pressure on my lungs. During soccer games I'd often run with my hand under my shirt to do this, hoping the coach wouldn't see me struggling and take me out of the game.

Once I started taking Cromolyn and Ventolin for treatment, my growth stunted. When I was finally able to wean off the Cromolyn, I began to grow a little again, but then my knees started hurting all the time. During baseball games, I remember putting my hands on my knees while waiting for a flyball and feeling them creak with pain. It actually felt like fluid was gurgling through my kneecaps. *It couldn't be so, could it?* Doctors said it was growing pains, but I wasn't growing much, and the pain never stopped.

Fortunately, one day while riding my bike, a car veered into the wrong lane and ran me off the road, catapulting me into the bumper of a parked car. The impact was so severe that I cracked the bumper in half with my left knee, but at the hospital, instead of a break, X-rays revealed an unusual bone disease called osteochondritis. An X-ray of the other knee revealed the same problem. The disease had worn away two nickel-sized holes in my kneecaps, ultimately giving me years of arthritic pain.

To fix me, they put one leg in a full-length cast and made me walk around in the dorkiest way possible for months. I wanted to walk like a jock with a broken ankle, where you balance on one foot and thrust both crutches forward, but instead I had to walk around like a soldier doing the goosestep, each crutch falling in line with the opposite leg. All I wanted was to be a normal, healthy kid, and it drove me crazy that I seemed to be the only one of my classmates dealing with chronic health issues. Now I couldn't even get to use crutches the cool way. It felt like I was missing out. I hated the idea of missing out. This was when the little Napoleon inside me was born. Between puffs of Ventolin and walking around on crutches, I developed an intense need for living a life unencumbered, and a fear of living a life unfulfilled. Sometimes that fear made me do some pretty stupid stuff.

There was that time when I was twelve and a friend and I thought it would be smart to test out the December ice in Scituate Harbor. We fell in and my friend nearly lost his life. There was also that lapse in judgment when I was twenty-one, and bungee jumping outside a bar in Mexico at two in the morning seemed like a perfectly reasonable idea. It didn't even give me pause when the "attendants" stuffed newspapers into the ankle harnesses to ensure a secure fit. Worse, though, was that time when I was a ski instructor in Telluride, attempting one last 360-degree jump for the day. After twelve failed attempts, I was tired and done, but one of my friends kept saying, "Come on Matt, you are getting closer than anybody. Just try one more time. You are totally going to get it." One more time resulted in a compression fracture of the T7 disc in my spine; a mistake I'm still paying for today.

But my fear of regrets also led me to move back to Boston on the off-chance I would reconnect with the one woman I ever really loved. (I did, and she married me. Ka-chow!) It also led me on four cross-country driving trips, countless overnight sailing adventures, and the chance to study in Spain. It even took me on a backpacking trip across Europe, with hardly any money in my pocket, before compelling me to live in five different states in my twenties and saying yes to more adventures than my body was probably ready to absorb. Then it got me to start a business and go back to grad school to make sure I knew what the hell I was doing. The point is, my fear of regrets gets me moving and has been a key factor in leading me up every mountain I have ever climbed. That and the little angry Napoleon inside of me who is fighting for the minutes.

Many moons ago, at a Christmas dinner with my extended family, some of my relatives expressed their regrets about the many things they wished they had done when they were younger, but never did. I was twenty-two at the time, and their idle conversation struck a chord. They sounded trapped. Like life was preordained and that their options for adventure were limited because they were now deeply rooted in society's fold. It scared the hell out of me. I didn't want to be sitting at a table someday, speaking of regrets, so I made a promise to myself that night to act upon my impulses. It was the first time I formalized in my mind what had already been a lifetime fear.

I'm quite sure none of my relatives remember this night and thought nothing of the conversation. My dad, who remembers everything, has no recollection of it, so that's my proof it was an altogether meaningless discussion at the dinner table, having no real bearing on anyone's true regrets or choices. But such is life. Across the world meaningless conversations are taking place right now that affect nobody in the room except one, because it means something entirely different for them. Seemingly meaningless conversations have butterfly effects that lead people to all sorts of places.

Chapter 12

Lock-steps

I only recently turned thirty-nine, but skiing out west was my fortieth birthday present to myself. In my humble opinion, there's no better place to ski than Utah in March, so my college buddies and I were heading to Park City, the largest ski area in the United States after Vail Resorts recently merged it with the Canyons. Bully for us. I booked the house and the plan was set. Six of us made the trip and it wasn't only what I needed; every one of the guys said they had been needing something like this. We skied Thursday to Sunday, and over the course of those four days I heard all of them say things like: "Why haven't we been doing this every year?" and "Where are we going next year?" These were great questions.

But Matt, you may ask, *how do you pull off leaving your wife and kids for four days to do this?* Well, I'll tell you. First, you need to either have a cool wife, or a wife who is susceptible to the peer pressure of other cool wives, so that she does the cool thing and lets you go on said trip. Fortunately, I have the former, so no gnashing of teeth there.

Second, you need to make sure you don't spend your money on stupid stuff like infomercial dicers or another hundred-dollar Lego set. Have you seen the prices on Legos lately? There is no doubt in my mind that the single biggest thing bringing down the middle class in the United States isn't China or Mexico, but the thousands of dollars' worth of Legos scattered around living rooms across the country. Someone needs to look into the toll Legos are having on our nation.

Having stepped on one too many Legos in the middle of the night, Liz and I now save most of our money for travel. A trip to Utah, therefore, wasn't a challenging discussion, because she knows I save for it, and she wants to give me these opportunities as long as it doesn't create any financial stress. Which brings me to the third and most critical recipe for taking a guy trip without marital repercussions—separate checking accounts.

The year before we were married, Liz was working for a hedge fund company in San Francisco, while I was a Financial Consultant with Wells Fargo. During that time, even though she was making more money than me, I insisted on paying all of the bills, my feeling being that at some point we would be married and someday, hopefully, have children. When that day came, I wanted us to be able to depend exclusively on my income, so that Liz had the choice, if she wanted it, to stay home with the kids. It was important to me that I get myself into the habit of making sure we could financially handle the ups and downs of life, without her salary to lean upon, should life require it.

Everything went fine with this plan until we got married. Following our wedding, Liz insisted we get a joint checking account. I think a lot of her college friends advised her to do this because they had heard some horror stories and they wanted Liz to have the security that I wasn't playing fast and loose with what was now OUR money. I think her father advised her to do it as well, probably because I wasn't a trusted entity yet. Whatever the reason, insist upon a joint checking account she did, and when I went to pay our bills that month, for the first time in my life, every check bounced.

I was horrified. My whole life I had lived in fear of bouncing checks, and now I had bounced four or five in less than a week. As a rule, I usually kept a few thousand in my checking account to ensure I could cover anything that required a big outlay, LIKE RENT. *The last time I checked the account there was over two thousand dollars in there!* Where did it go? Was I a victim of identity theft?

I came to find out that while I was getting into the habit of saving money to pay bills, Liz was getting into the habit of spending every dollar in her checking account. She could do this, guilt free, because she maxed out her 401(k) contributions with every paycheck. When our checking accounts merged, she did what she always did and drew the account down to zero, not realizing I liked to transfer in a reserve balance for paying bills. That was the first time I realized I needed to work on my communication skills. In our second month of marriage we went back to separate checking accounts, and have never had an argument about money again: she is free to do what she wants with what she saves, and me the same. It's beautiful.

Therefore, with no money debate to be had, I was free to go on a trip to Utah with my pals. Liz not only accepted it, but encouraged it, giving me advice on where to go and where to stay. She knew I needed it. I'm so bad about making time to hang out with friends during the year, it's better if I get all of my "me time" in during one four-day splurge. Plus, she goes on her own ski trip each year with her girlfriends, so, quid pro quo.

Skiing at Park City was great. We carved turns over every trail, grabbed pints at every tavern with animal heads hanging from the walls, and laughed as much as we did in college. It was awesome. A couple days into the adventure though, it was clear that I wasn't the only one grappling with the idea of turning forty, and somewhere in our collective subconscious was an awareness that our ability to challenge our age was diminished by the fact that we were using chairlifts to ski. Given my current quest to bag the 4000-footers, my mind was bent on seeing if there were any good places to hike up and ski down. The fellas wanted to do the same.

On the Canyons side of Park City, way to the right if you are looking up from the base, sits Murdock Peak. Hopping off the Super Condor Express chair, the play is to muster up as much speed as you can and launch yourself up Murdock Peak as far as possible before stepping out of your bindings to climb. Hoisting our skis on our shoulders, we came upon a friendly woman in her sixties who said she had hiked up Murdock many times before, but was too tired to attempt it with us today. We offered our sympathies and without further hesitation, turned and marched up the peak in quick-step fashion. My pals, some of whom looked in better shape than me, fell behind as they struggled to make clean steps in the deep snow. In some places we sunk in all the way down to our waists.

When I reached the summit, I realized that all of my winter hiking had made me an efficient climber, and I was reminded of something I learned while climbing Mount Rainier. On Rainier, the snow was extremely deep, and the weight of the fifty-pound packs made the climb the most arduous I've ever endured. During the climb, our guide told me about "lock-steps," also known as rest-steps, where you make each step deliberately and methodically, and literally lock your knee under you as you complete each step. This relieves muscle strain as you utilize more of your skeleton to support the effort. It sounds simple, but it really works, and is something I do almost unconsciously now on steep ascents. I called down to my buddy Ed and told him about lock-steps. Immediately, his gait improved, and when he reached the top, he echoed my sentiments about the benefits of such a simple tip.

It was only an hour-long hike up, maybe less, but looking out from 9600 feet over the Wasatch Range—sugar coated mountains as far as the eye can see—our collective youth was restored. We smiled at each other, quietly proud of the group and our friendship. We felt like men again, whatever that means. You could see it on everyone's faces. As we drank in the moment and caught our breath, the sweat started to ice our brows and chill our necks, prompting us to get moving and collect our reward: fresh tracks in some epic pow-pow!

Picking my line, floating up and down the pillowy snow, I could hear my friends giggling all around me. My buddies Mike and Pat appeared at my side, their turns working in concert with mine, and in that moment I was relieved of any responsibility I had on this planet, free of the name Matt Larson and all that he has to do; I was just a being, simple and light, dancing on marshmallow sand.

The next day, hoping to sustain the excitement, we hiked up Scott's Bowl, which is on the Iron Mountain side of the resort. The joy of another conquest brought about more giggles, but it was hard to replicate the same jubilation. The snow was still incredible and everywhere we looked there were opportunities to paint new lines on the canvas before us, but we were slipping from euphoria into contentment. Our purpose had been served. We had reclaimed our bond and spurned the monotony of regular life. Forty was approaching and we had said something about it.

Chapter 13

It's the Climb

At the foot of Passaconaway is a homestead with a long gray barn in great working order, though no work was happening this chilly April morning. Grassy fields in the foreground, surfacing from the winter snows, carried a sandy-gold hue—the kind that appears after the final haying of the autumn season. If it wasn't for the sunny blue skies, you would have sworn it was November. When I arrived, mine was the only car at the designated parking area and I felt a tingle as I struck up phase two of my journey. *The first car here!*

After a full month since my last ascent, I was anxious to get started again. Mountain cravings were a daily problem for me now, and the long reprieve had me starving to get some peaks into my system. Wishful thinking prompted me to schedule another work meeting for after the climb, but this hike was going to be different—somewhere between eleven and fifteen miles—my intention being to use it as a training hike for harder days to come. In addition to two 4000-footers, the route included four smaller mountains to summit, making it a six-peak day in total. As such, I knew there was a good chance I wouldn't be able to make my afternoon meeting. Now I can't even remember what the meeting was for.

A mile in, huffing and buckling under the weight of my pack, I reined myself in and started eating my first apple of the day. The longer trek and variable weather required a lot of water and extra gear, and the additional load was having an obvious effect. Pausing to look around, I noted how quiet it was. *A little too quiet.* This was the first climb where there wasn't any snow on the ground, and it dawned on me that bears might be waking up soon. *If they haven't already!* Suddenly my winter confidence evaporated and I felt like a squirrel trapped inside a cabin; my eyes widened and my tail twitched. I ceased masticating and halted in the middle of the trail, listening. There was nothing but silence. No birds. No chipmunks rustling through the underbrush. *Well, this is weird.*

In the winter I loved the silence, was even rejuvenated by it. But now it felt . . . off. Somewhere in the constructs of my mind I determined that all forest animals go quiet with fear if a bear is around, so certainly, a bear must be nearby. I think I learned this from watching Disney cartoons. After a few minutes of earnestly pointing my ears in every direction, I started back up again at a cautious pace, spooked out and on the alert. Slow-stepping my way up the slope, I scanned ahead for black moving shapes, but nothing was there. I scanned behind me. Nothing there either. I went on like this for a couple hundred feet, repeatedly checking ahead, side to side, and then behind. Finally, I began to relax. After one last look over my shoulder, I turned my attention back to my apple and resumed my normal pace. That's when they attacked.

From the depths of an oversized barberry bush came an explosion of pain and fury, the likes of which I had never heard before. A cacophony of screams, whistles, and slapping noises erupted all at once, like thunder clapping during the middle of a cannon fire assault. My heart froze and I ducked. Bodies came hurtling out of the bush, buzzsawing the air a few feet from my face, and I craned my head back to avoid getting hit.

"HOLY SHIT!" I yelled at the mass of pheasants blasting upwards. Or were they quail? I jumped back and thrust my arms out like an officer halting oncoming traffic. "Holy shit!" I shouted again, my eyes darting back and forth from sky to bush, as more enemy combatants emerged, their wings beating inexorably in every direction. They just kept coming. Apparently, every living pheasant in the state of New Hampshire had decided to ambush me from this single bush as part of some big outdoorsy joke. As the last quail emerged from his hiding place, I stared after it for a moment before shouting, "What the hell?!" And then once again for good measure, "HOLY SHIT!"

I took a minute to regain my composure before continuing along the path, no longer scared of bears; I was sure that every bear within a five-mile radius skedaddled after that hullabaloo. Caution waning, my steps quickened, and I briskly made my way up the trail until strips of ice appeared. Needing no time to deliberate, I grabbed my microspikes and strapped them on. Gone were the days of fooling around, trying to see how far I could go without needing them. Now I was a weapon of hiking efficiency, deftly maneuvering around any obstacle on my intense journey towards finding relaxed sanctuary.

Approaching the summit of Wonalancet, I came across a stone ledge covered in ferns. Greenery hadn't taken root anywhere else, not even on the soil around it. Only on that rock. I couldn't make sense of it until I saw the sun tickling its way through the trees above, managing to concentrate its full strength on the ferns in front of me. Feeling a little Muir-esque, I sat down to watch the sun kiss the earth and observe the passing of time. I imagined the rock exhaling in thanks.

Years ago, when I first read John Muir, I had a hard time believing he didn't do just a little bit of drugs. Listen to this sentence he wrote: "When I discovered a new plant, I sat down beside it for a minute or a day, to make its acquaintance and hear what it had to tell . . . I asked the boulders I met, whence they came and whither they were going." I mean, who asks rocks where they are going? Once I went to a party where some guy spent the evening laying down in the backyard, rubbing dirt all over himself and talking to the trees. I think he also said something about being a chicken. The guy was tripping on shrooms, completely out of his mind, and acting, perhaps, a little Muir-esque.

But even though I have always been a big nature guy, until climbing the 4000-footers, I always found Muir's writing a little too "out there." Reading about his trips into Yosemite Valley, I'm often reminded of Keifer Sutherland's character in *Young Guns*, high as a kite on peyote, talking about how "she's my flower and I'm her butterfly." When Muir doesn't sound high, he sounds removed, as if he has found the answer to all of life's greatest questions that we mere mortals would be hard-pressed to understand. I always felt that if I ever met Muir, I'd find him very hard to talk to. But after spending so much time alone in the mountains, I was starting to have these moments where I felt the earth more firmly. More completely. As if I were melting into it. With each climb, Muir's writing made more and more sense.

Edward Abbey's writing came much easier to me. The first time I read *Desert Solitaire*, I connected with it, and immediately felt the call of the wilderness. Ironically, Abbey openly discussed his drug use in some of his writing and lived a life of bachelorhood that I couldn't envision attempting, yet his writing is so remarkably down-to-earth, you feel right there with him. While Muir sounds removed from society, having already discovered life's truths, Abbey seems embedded in the search for truth, waging war with society and its rules. For me, he is a part of the world, *and* removed from it, trying to mold out a new method of living that incorporates people with the spiritual beauty of the outdoors. This I can relate to. Give me Abbey. Sorry John.

Of course, maybe I don't understand either of them too well. Abbey comes off a little strange, better suited for the company of Hunter S. Thompson than anyone I would enjoy spending time with. But despite his ramblings (something I would never do, no), his writing takes you to an earthlier plane, connecting you to the trials and tribulations of life among people, even when he is off wandering deep into the National Park System as a ranger. Muir, on the other hand, appears to be dancing among the stars, creating imagery of the planet below that no brush can paint. *Sigh*. Maybe Muir's love for nature simply far outshines my own, as I was only able to sit and observe the sun moving across the rocks for thirty minutes or so. In my defense, I didn't have more time to spare.

I'm sure Muir would not approve of me spending my time pursuing a list of mountains to "bag." I imagine he'd object to the idea of itemizing the world around us and find the exercise a triviality that devalues the experience of communing with nature. But hey, Muir also left his wife for years at a time to go play in the woods and wander around like a billy goat with nothing but some bread and nuts to subsist on. Admirable, inspiring, and not wholly reasonable for anybody to emulate. Kind of weird, frankly.

Sure, following a list is not a very romantic way to connect with nature, but it sure is helpful in explaining to people what you're doing. If I was taking off at 4am one day every week to go find random rocks to talk to, they might lock me up and throw away the key. But tackling a list? Especially one as well known as the 4000-footer list? This is something people can get behind. The 4000-footer list is understandable, because ours is a culture of lists, and each day presents a set of tasks you need to tackle. Get to work. Pay the bills. Spend time with the in-laws. Drive the kids to their ever-growing hobbies. Feed the dog. Put up the Christmas lights. Go to dinner with that new couple your wife just met with the husband who you're supposed to really like but don't. Go to the dump. Fix this. Fix that. Feed the dog again. *Hey, has anyone fed the fish this month?*

But with the 4000-footers, instead of adding another thing to your "real" life list, you are working on a to-do list for the soul. It's a list designed for fulfillment, rather than "have-tos." Using the inclination to task-orient your life, a peakbagging list allows you to trick yourself into starting off on the path of getting something done, only to find that you have no choice but to slow down and enjoy the experience. There's no way around it. No, literally—you're climbing a mountain, so there's no way around it. And there is nothing like a long climb to make you appreciate the reasons you cared to make all those annoying and tedious life lists you're escaping from. Climbing over Hibbard and then Nanamocomuck, I thought about Liz and the kids, my friends and my family, and smiled. Those mundane life lists had purpose again. Then I smiled because I was getting to climb something called Nanamocomuck. It's fun just saying it. How many people even know this mountain exists?

The best part about a peakbagging list is that it makes your life lists more tolerable. You never want to think of the things you have to do for your wife or your children as chores. Work is a chore enough. Once the people you love become facets of the monotonous burden of getting things done, you jeopardize your relationship with them and the love you have for them. Squeezing in time for yourself is critical for loving others, and a peakbagging list gives you a framework to find some "me time" without having to dwell too long on how to get it. The 4000-footer list is really a freedom list, designed to give you space and time to expand yourself.

Naturally, finding the time for a personal peakbagging list requires you to arrange your life a certain way. You need to be able to get up early and stay physically fit. Although not too fit. I made all of my climbs with extra pounds on my paunch, so you don't have to be some extreme parkour junkie. Plenty of overweight senior citizens haul themselves up and down these mountains as well, so it's not like this is too, too hard. If you are going to do them all in a year, though, you probably need to be able to run a few miles without throwing up.

To climb in the small hours of the morning, I also found that you can't drink that much. Or eat crappy food. I hate to give up ice cream, but my buddy Jonathan always insisted that ice cream was the worst thing to have the night before a big run or a physically challenging adventure, and he was totally right. If I ate ice cream or had a few beers the night before a climb, I always felt a dramatic weight on my performance, pun intended. Without ice cream or beer in my belly from the night before, I traveled light and fast, and I took note of this, gratefully, when I reached the top of Passaconaway.

Plopping down for a rest, I dropped my feet over the cliff's edge to fully immerse myself in the surroundings. From my perch I could see Lake Winnipesaukee, shimmering in the morning sun, and Gunstock's ski trails in the distance. Wrestling with the desire to bag Whiteface, but also stay and admire the scenery, I ate half of a peanut butter and jelly sandwich to force myself to slow down and be in the moment.

The singing bug hit me when I departed Passaconaway's summit, this time a song called "Bedside Window." Ambling over the ice, I gently sang, "and the rain, it cooled our bodies, burned by a love too warm." Catching glimpses of Whiteface through the trees as I made my way, I felt exalted. Nothing could ruin this day. "Our tears, and sweat, made mellow, while the leaves, from the trees, were torn." *God, that's a good song.* "Oh, there was a window by my bedside—AHHHH!" Right as I was getting into the final chorus, the ground came out from under me and hit me in the rear. Before I could react, I started sliding down a luge of ice. Five feet. Ten feet. Fifteen. With nothing to grab on to, it was a little scary, but I managed to get my feet out in front of me and ram them into a fallen tree, my microspikes digging into its bark. My knees buckled upon impact and were already stiff with pain when I stood up. *Owwww.*

Twenty minutes later, the pain in my rear subsided, but my kneecaps still felt like bricks scraping against my femurs. There was nothing for it. The closest path to the car was a three-hour hike over Whiteface, so I had no option but to trudge on. Somehow, whether it was the views or the sweet smell of the air, I eventually forgot about my pain. It was still there, but compartmentalized by the inescapable need to climb.

Some spots of the trail were pure ice, while others had three feet of snow, making it difficult to manage without snowshoes. The frequent changes in trail conditions made switching back and forth between spikes and snowshoes a tedious exercise, so I opted to keep the spikes on and slog through waist-high snow when necessary. Once I got over my pain a little, I started moving a bit too quickly through a heavily wooded part of the trail and ran my face into a frigging tree branch. How I didn't see it coming, I couldn't tell you.

By the time I got back to my truck, I was a mess. My face was nicked with blood and two massive blisters had developed on my left foot. My knees and my ass needed Advil directly injected into them, and I was walking bowlegged. Bruises were running up and down my right arm, perhaps from the fall or the run in with the tree, I didn't know which. I was beat up, tired, worn down, and worn out. *And it felt great!* The views were lovely and all, but it was the hammering I took that had me feeling interminably alive. That was some climb.

When you reach the end of a goal you set for yourself, you may feel a great surge of accomplishment at first, knowing you did what you set out to do. But soon after, or a few months later, a void can develop. For so long you had a clear purpose and now you are adrift, wondering what to do next. You need to find another purpose and it becomes clear that it's not the achievement that sustains you. It's not the summit. Whenever I look back on a climb, it's always the challenges and the effort I recall more fondly than the views from the summit itself. It's the climb that fills my being. The spirit lifts knowing it is on a path to somewhere—anywhere—because movement leads to learning and learning leads to growth.

Chapter 14

The Gift

When I was seventeen my dad took me to Africa to climb Mount Kilimanjaro. Before this the only "mountains" we had ever climbed together were Red Hill and West Rattlesnake, two hills situated in the New Hampshire Lakes Region. And we hadn't climbed those since I was ten. But in typical Don fashion, if you are going to do something, you better go big, and he decided that before I headed off to college, we needed a male bonding trip. It was the greatest gift he ever gave me and one of the best parenting decisions he's ever made.

Before the climb, we got to enjoy an African safari, concentrated around the Serengeti and the Ngorongoro Crater. It was wild. On one of our first nights, situated in a thickly forested area, a commotion arose from the trees lining the perimeter of our camp, and our guide told us to remain inside our tents, fearing it might be water buffalo—very dangerous. It turned out to be a much larger threat, as a herd of elephants tromped by, less than thirty feet from where we slept. On another night, camping out in the Serengeti, I had to get up to pee. Mid-effort, I spotted two green eyes, low to the ground, staring back at me through the darkness. Baboons hung around the campsite dumpster, and I reasoned it must be one of them, but this fellow was entirely content to remain motionless, unlike any of the baboons I met. *What if those eyes are low because they belong to a crouching lion?* Not wanting to risk it, I broke stream and hurried back into my tent.

In 1994 there was nothing but dirt roads in northern Tanzania, nor much in the way of services. In the villages, scores of shoeless kids surrounded our vehicles, looking for treats, while women walked by balancing wicker baskets on their heads. Homes and shops constructed of aluminum Coca-Cola signs lined the streets of ever-present mud, where weathered men sat under lean-to shelters, waiting to trade their goods. When our jeep broke down, the guide had no choice but to fix it himself. When we needed to go to the bathroom, we went outside, or if lucky enough to find one, in a seatless outhouse. The contrast to American life was astonishing.

Along the way, we met a Masai tribe who liked trading beads for goods. Evidently, on a previous trip, some American asshole traded a Confederate flag with them, and the Masai, unaware of its significance, raised it twenty feet above their village on a reed pole for all the world to see.

While still digesting the irony of that image as we entered the settlement, some of the tribe's warriors invited me into their hut.

Inside was pitch dark and breathing was difficult on account of the smoldering fire in the center of the room, its smoke having nowhere to escape through the mud and thatch roof. My eyes burned and I could hardly see a thing. A picture developed after the trip (because these were the days of film) showed an image of my companions and me squinting painfully at the camera; evidence that I wasn't the only one who was uncomfortable. But back outside the hut, the Masai were cheerful and engaging, apparently ok with their living situation. I was in awe.

Everywhere we went there was something amazing and new to behold, but nothing was quite like seeing Kilimanjaro for the first time. Standing at 19,341 feet, Kilimanjaro is the tallest mountain in Africa. One of the Seven Summits, it rises from the earth as if by magic. There's nothing to explain its height. There are no other mountains surrounding it to suggest a smashing up of the earth. It simply stands there by itself, dominating the landscape.

Our climbing party had two guides. The leader of the team was Jacob, who years later went on to appear in the IMAX film titled *Kilimanjaro: To the Roof of Africa.* Accompanying him was a younger guide, whose name escapes me now, although I want to say it was Winston. The rest of our group consisted of a couple in their early sixties, a young Australian man of about thirty-three who was trying to figure out what he was going to do with the rest of his life, and my friend RJ and his dad Chip.

The first day of the climb took us through the jungle, and RJ and I camped together that night. The next day when we woke, feeling strong and sure-footed, we took off with the younger guide and motored up to the 11,000-foot mark where the next camp was located. All was well until 2am, when RJ got up to answer nature's call. Upon his exit, my stomach did a somersault, and I bolted upright in my sack.

The world was spinning. I tried to reach out and unzip the tent, but I was so dizzy that I couldn't focus well enough to find the zipper. Feebly, I uttered, "RJ, hurry. Open the tent." The sound of my voice was so weak, I doubted he would hear me, but he did. Unfortunately, it was too late. As he started fumbling with the zipper from the outside, I said, "hurry" again, and then let loose a stream of projectile vomit with such force that it tore a hole through the tent wall. I think I may have even gotten a little on RJ. I had never felt so bad in my life.

My head felt like a train was running through it. After vomiting until all of my organs were strewn out before me, my dad switched spots with RJ in our tent so he could monitor me for the rest of the night. He asked if I could lie down, but I couldn't. Every time I turned my head I threw up. If I tried to lie down, I threw up. All I could do was sit and look forward, rocking my body ever so gently, and close my eyes.

In the morning we consulted Jacob on what to do. Usually in these situations they leave the ailing climber behind to wait for the rest of the party to return from the summit, but Jacob suggested that we see how I felt after a little bit of hot iodine tea. The first cup I threw up, but the second one seemed to hold. When I was finally able to step out of the tent and keep my feet, Jacob approached me and said, "halloo Matayoo."

Trying to look at him without my head exploding was like trying to stare directly into the sun without going blind. He pointed at a giant headwall farther up the trail and explained that this was my primary job for the day: if I could climb it, maybe I could be allowed to continue with the rest of the climb. My dad took my pack to carry and gave me his windbreaker, since I had thrown up on most of my own stuff. All I needed to worry about was walking and trying not to hurl.

I had never heard of altitude sickness before this, but the consensus was that the rapid speed with which RJ and I ascended had gotten to me. I've seen others experience altitude sickness since, and the symptoms range all over the place. Some people have trouble seeing or get shortness of breath. Others have blinding headaches that can't be staunched for days. For me it felt like the worst case of food poisoning ever.

I spent the day inching along the trail, taking little half steps to avoid jostling my head too much. If my head felt the slightest jiggle, I wanted to barf. I spit up a couple more times, but it was only bile now. We took several breaks, and each time we did, I'd collapse into the same sitting position I held all night long in the tent. It was impossible to tip my head without inducing nausea, so there was no chance of lying down. Hiking over the barren approach to Kilimanjaro, I barely noticed what lay before me. All I could do was keep my eyes on the ground, concentrate on sipping my iodine water, and conserve my energy by not uttering a word to anyone. It was a very long day.

The next day I fared a little bit better. I still couldn't stomach any food, but the headache was subsiding, and it started to look like I might have a shot at managing this thing. Jacob instructed me to go "poli-poli," which in Swahili meant "slowly," and I didn't argue. I couldn't manage any other speed. By the time we got into camp that night, I was so tired I couldn't even pull the boots off my feet. I remember my dad helping me out of them before I collapsed into my sleeping bag. I was so thankful to be able to finally lay down without vomiting, and for this man who was willing to look after me. I had never loved him so much.

My dad and I had always been pretty close, with the inevitable temporary distance that grows between a father and son during the teenage years, but throughout my childhood I never considered him tender. He could be nice, and funny, and fun, but this man, who was willing to help me out of my clothes and walk step for step with me up the largest mountain in Africa, no matter how slowly I moved, was something new to me. I could feel him watching me as I struggled up the slopes, sipping my water. He looked at me with concern and care, without ever voicing his worry. Years later I realized that there was nothing new about this. That in Africa I was simply witnessing the physical manifestation of him climbing with me my whole life. Looking back at it, I think the way he handled Kilimanjaro was the bravest thing he ever did, and I'm amazed how he kept it together. Being a father now myself, I think I'd be scared as hell to watch my son throw up all night in a tent in the middle of Africa, miles away from civilization and any hospital. He must have been scared some, but he never showed it.

On the last day of the ascent, we got up in the dark and watched the sun come up as we made our way to a highpoint called "Stella's Point," six hundred feet shy of Uhuru Peak, which is the top of Kilimanjaro. We stopped there for one last rest before the summit, and Jacob warned me not to close my eyes. At such altitudes people were known to fall asleep and never wake up, he said. I promised him I wouldn't and then closed my eyes when he wasn't looking.

When we got up to make our final push, my dad put his arm around me and said, "You know, you don't have to keep going if you want to stop. As far as I'm concerned, you climbed this mountain." But there was no way I was going to stop now. You can't come all the way to Africa, get yourself a few hundred feet shy of the summit, and then turn around! For the last three days, the thought that I could come all the way to Africa, and not make summit, was more unbearable than the churning in my stomach and the pounding in my head. I was going to summit.

From the top of Kilimanjaro, I reached back and spit. It wasn't a "I spit on you" spit, but more of a return to sender kind of spit. I didn't give it much thought; it was guttural. Just one good strong spit to say: I saw what you had to give me, I took it, you gave it your best shot, and I beat you. Looking out from Uhuru Peak, I was overcome with the knowledge that if I could do this, against significant odds, there was nothing I couldn't do. Climbing Kilimanjaro gave me the internal belief that from that day forward, whenever I faced one of life's many challenges—a big test, getting into college, public speaking, getting a job, planning for my future—I could handle it. Life's problems seemed so much smaller from then on. But that lesson, that learning, may have never happened if my dad hadn't let me see it through.

It took some serious courage to let me go forward, considering the state I was in. Maybe it was our naiveté about the dangers of altitude sickness that allowed us to continue, and I'm sure nowadays there are plenty who would say that our decision was reckless. But clearly, I was capable, and my dad had made an accurate assessment, and continuous reassessment, of my ability to proceed. The faith that he showed me on that trip was the best gift I have ever received from him. By giving me the chance to prove myself, I happened to prove to myself that I was capable of anything. That's a gift that keeps on giving.

On the descent, Dad came up to me again, put his arm around me and said, "Matthew, I am so touched you just did that. So fricking touched." His voice was shaky with pride and his hug made me feel warm. He hadn't hugged me like that since I was a little kid. It was the first hint of emotion I caught from him during the whole climb, and it capped off the greatest vacation I ever had.

Look, I get it. Puking your brains out and feeling nauseous for days, completely unable to eat while climbing a nineteen-thousand-foot mountain in Africa, doesn't sound like a dream vacation. But to this day, when people ask me what the best trip I ever took was, I tell them about Kilimanjaro. Because on Kilimanjaro I walked up to its summit a boy and descended a man.

When we returned to base camp there were only five of our original party left: the older couple had turned around on the third day. They weren't the fittest pair, and the effort proved to be too much for them, so they left for home. It was a wise choice; at base we learned that members of another climbing party had died a day or two before we set out. The cause wasn't exactly clear, but with dangers like that, there's no point in taking unnecessary risks, right? *Um, yeah.*

As we parted company with our guides and the porters who helped lug the cooking gear up the mountain, Dad gave Jacob his red winter jacket. Freezing our butts off on the last day of the ascent, Dad couldn't believe that Jacob made this trek time and again without proper outerwear. It's always customary to tip your climbing guide, but Dad felt that in this case, cash wasn't enough. "You need a good jacket," he told Jacob, as Jacob laughed.

Years later, watching the IMAX film about Kilimanjaro, it was surreal to see and hear Jacob again, leading another team up the mountain. I was transported. The film was a remarkably accurate depiction of the experience, and as Jacob appeared on the screen during his opening monologue, I was glad to see that he was, in fact, wearing a good jacket. I can't believe it was the same one Dad gave him, but it was red, so who knows. Wherever he got it from, he deserved it, to say the least. Jacob—wherever you are and wherever you go, thank you.

Chapter 15

Lost and Found

Six days after Whiteface and Passaconaway, I was back at it again, gunning to get at least halfway done with the list before summer started. Time was ticking. I woke up at 2am with a sore throat, either from eating too much pizza the night before, allergy season kicking in, or some other weird illness I always seem to get every other week. Typical. Nonetheless, I got up and hit the road, and even managed to get a little work done before reaching the trailhead at 5:45.

Mount Osceola was the day's objective, but when I arrived at the Tripoli Road exit—the access point to the Osceola trailhead—it was still closed for the winter. Osceola had been on my mind ever since failing my first attempt at it, long before I became wise to the ways of winter hiking. But now that I was finally equipped with spikes and ready for it, it wasn't ready for me. Spurned by Osceola yet again and not wanting to waste any time, I picked an alternate peak to bag and quick. Consulting my trusty Peakbagger app, I surveyed what was nearby. The access point to the Flume Slide Trail was only a little farther up the highway and just like that, my decision was made for me; I set my eyes on Flume and Liberty. Suddenly, what was supposed to be a one peak day was going to be a double bagger!

Unfortunately, I was already exhausted and could hardly keep my eyes open by the time I pulled into the Flume parking area. *This is dumb.* In a couple days I was taking my family on vacation to the Grand Canyon, and I was probably going to make myself sick trying to squeeze these two mountains in. My sore throat started feeling worse from the worry.

Not to mention, the whole point of getting up this early was completely shot. Lately, I'd been getting into photography and wanted to start the day off by capturing some beautiful sunrise pictures in the mountains. I've always had a fondness for photography but my quest for the 4000-footers rekindled my love for it; the views are too magnificent not to record. As an added bonus, the new world of social media allowed me to share the beauty I found with other people, which I rather enjoyed. But there would be no sunrise pic to show my Instagram community today. With all the time wasted driving around to get to an alternate mountain, I missed my chance of getting an #epic

#sunrise shot, and all I cared about was taking a nap to get my energy back. #sosleepy.

And yes, I admit it. Even though I think a lot of social media is asinine, I kinda think Instagram is okay. Hear me out. You don't have to read anybody's captions if you don't want to—you can simply enjoy the pictures—and you won't offend your friends if you unfollow them because you're not interested in the pictures of the food they're eating. They won't even know if you unfollow them unless they have a private account and you try to follow them again later, which would be hella lame. (Do kids still say that? Did they ever?) Apparently my #instagame was pretty bad though, because my kids' babysitter, Alicia, decided she needed to coach me on the proper number, and types, of hashtags to use.

For starters, I didn't know what a hashtag was, so that needed to be explained to me several times. When I finally did use a hashtag, I learned that I was using the wrong ones, and too few of them. Overcompensating for my lack of social awareness, I then used way, way too many. *Matt, you can't use twenty hashtags. You need to cut that down to like five, tops.* To be #instacool, I think you are supposed to use no more than four hashtags, but no less than two. I'm not sure. My coach kept reprimanding me because I was still hovering around eight hashtags per post. Wanderingmatt8 still had lots to learn.

Too tired to pursue Instafame anyway, I cranked my seat back and closed my eyes, but sleep wouldn't come. All I could do was sit there and rest my thoughts. After five minutes my mind started churning again and I was too consciously aware of the sun beating through the windshield to wait any longer. By 6:05 I was out of the car and my feet were taking me back to where I belonged, following in the footsteps of Bill Bryson and Cheryl Strayed, and maybe to a lesser extent John Muir and Edward Abbey. Well, really only Bryson I guess, because I don't think any of the others climbed these mountains.

Speaking of Bryson, I love and hate his book *A Walk in the Woods*. I love his witty sense of humor and his commentary about the things he sees and the conversations he has. His writing is fantastic and I'm sure you've read it if you're willing to stick with me here. But I hate that he never finished the Appalachian Trail. And I loathe that he has a picture of a bear on the cover of his book when he NEVER SAW A BEAR THE ENTIRE TIME HE WAS ON THE TRAIL. The cover is a lie! You have to read the whole book until he admits on the last page or two that he never actually saw a bear at all. The whole cover makes you feel like you're going to read about a hilarious encounter with a bear, and . . .? There's no bear! Only anecdotes about other people's run-ins with bears. We were hoodwinked. I'm calling you out Bryson, for gross misrepresentation. Actually, my guess is that it was his publisher's idea so that they could sell more books. Clever. *Hmmm, I wonder if they'd publish me.*

There is one clear difference though between me and Bryson, and all of these other nature hound writers: they all dedicated huge swaths of time to their adventures, while yo-ho! I'm trying to squeeze this into what I've convinced myself is a balanced life. Who says I can't hold down a nine to five, be a dedicated father and husband, AND eat forty-eight mountains in a year? There's nothing wrong with trying to have it all, is there?

Everywhere you go, people are trying to have it all. It's not enough to go golfing on Saturdays anymore, no. Weekends are a torrent of activities packed with tennis, shows, cocktails, and cookouts. The more athletically inclined go mountain biking or run 5ks. If that doesn't satiate them, they run Spartan Races, Tough Mudders, Ironman Competitions, and some lunatics out there even do ultramarathons. If they aren't out adventuring, then they are off trying to win parent of the year awards by attending all of their kids' games. On Thursday nights, women may go out for drinks with their friends, where they concoct plans for a girl's weekend away. Not to be outdone, men are increasingly going on "mancations," where a group of buddies get together to reclaim their manhood for a weekend by skiing or doing some other activity together. *Hey, wait a second . . .*

Everyone seems to be taking trips they likely can't afford and saying "yes" to every plan that is pitched their way, determined to keep living life to the max. And who can blame them? What if this all ends tomorrow? What if I go into the doc's one day and he tells me I have cancer? Or six months to live? What if I get that news before I get to do all of the things I want to do?

Ever since forty started approaching, that Tim McGraw song "Live Like You Were Dying" kept finding me through the radio, torturing me. If you ever find yourself listening to it in your late thirties, you'll find it quite motivating, but also depressing as hell. Really, I can't listen to it for another second. It makes a great point though: you should live like you're dying because you've got no time to waste, and you will likely experience life and treat people better than you ever have before if you do. But lately I was noticing that living like I was dying, acquiring experiences at an ungodly rate, wasn't assuaging my fears of an untimely death. The temporary distractions of an action-packed life only helped to avoid the underlying issue. *Maybe,* I started thinking, *we're all biting off more than we should chew.*

When tackling the Liberty-Flume loop, most choose to summit Liberty first, opting for a more gradual ascent before descending the steeper Flume Slide Trail. But on this icy day, at this early hour, I thought it would be safer to go up the steeper route rather than trying to bumble my way down it after a long climb. I was also quite certain that I'd be alone on the trail if I ascended Flume first, so I didn't have to be too casual about an inevitable trail concert performance. Before I reached the halfway point of the ascent, I started feeling my usual mountain lift and let loose the first song that popped into my mind: "WHOAAOO, sweet darling, you took a piece of my heart, you took a piece of my heart. WHOOOAAAOOO . . ." The show had begun. One song followed another and before long, only music occupied my mind. I wasn't even aware of my steps.

Lost in my revelry, I managed to become lost on the trail, running smack into a dead-end marked by a thicket of bushes. I couldn't see where I went wrong. After leading me across a river, the trail completely vanished. *Where the heck did it go?* I hoped my ViewRanger app, courtesy of the expanding smartphone universe, would help me pick it up again, but I couldn't get a signal. Without technological support to guide me, I decided to bushwhack up the hill for another minute, where I stumbled upon some disgusting gray boxer briefs hanging from a tree. They were tattered and riddled with holes, looking like they were hung out to dry by some wild-eyed hobo. *This can't be right.* If someone was willing to get undressed over here, this couldn't be part of the tried-and-true trail. *Head back to the river.*

ViewRanger started working as I double-backed, and I used the in-app compass to point me towards the trail. Only every time ViewRanger said I was close to finding the trail again, I kept bumping back into the river. *What's going on here?* After thirty minutes of scraping my way through the woods, I realized that ViewRanger must have identified the river as the trail itself, and I was probably heading farther away from the trail with every step. I stopped and looked across the river. Crossing the river got me into this mess, maybe crossing it again would get me out.

During my zigzagging, I stubbornly kept my microspikes on because of one icy patch I slipped on twenty minutes earlier. But once I strapped them on, I didn't come across a single speck of ice. *Murphy's Law.* Instead of taking them off, I mucked my way through the mud and leaves before scraping my way back across the river rocks, aware of the damage I was doing to them but caring less. Thirty seconds after crossing back over the river, I found the turn in the trail I somehow missed before, all because I was too busy singing. What had led me astray was a well-trod area where other hikers stopped to dab their hands in the water and reflect. My big mistake was trying to bushwhack my way out of my predicament. What I should have done, and knew I should have done, was stop, retrace my steps, and return to the original trail. Regretfully, I don't always follow my own advice.

At the summit of Flume are some of the best panoramic views I've seen. Getting lost, slopping through the mud, and exerting extra effort to recover the trail was a pain, but views like these always make the effort worthwhile. Spread out before me was Franconia State Park, with Mount Pemigewasset and the Kinsman peaks in the distance. Liberty was waiting for me off to the right along the ridgeline. I climbed to the highest rock outcropping and took account of what I had done, contemplating how mountains have marked some of the most significant moments in my life. As I felt the wind and sun meet each other on the summit surface, it finally occurred to me that all of this—the need to climb now, the concern about turning forty, the recognition that time is fleeting—was predominantly about trying to find some grace as I transitioned into the second half of my life. Graceful purpose, to be exact.

On the way to Liberty's summit, I bumped into a woman in her fifties who took stock of my mountaineering sunglasses, the same ones I climbed Kilimanjaro with in 1994. With arms that wraparound my ears and goggle-sized lenses, they kind of make me look like a giant bug, and I have taken plenty of flak about them over the years. "Nice glasses!" she greeted. "Those are awesome. I wish I had something like them up here." *Yes! I knew they were cool!* The unexpected complement gave me a chuckle and a burst of energy. I practically skipped the rest of the way up to Liberty.

The summit of Liberty was the sixteenth of my quest; I was a third of the way done. Biting off that much of the 4000-footer list felt noteworthy, and I honored the moment by taking a long sit. Enjoying the view while I ate, I scanned the ridgeline from whence I came and could see why the Flume Slide Trail got its name. Rock scree and boulders funnel down the west side of the peak in sharp contrast to the pines buffering its sides, giving the appearance of an active rockslide. It didn't look fun to tackle in either direction. *Maybe that's why Lafayette and Lincoln are more popular than Flume and Liberty; maybe the trails are a little easier.* It had been so long since I had climbed Lafayette, I couldn't remember. All I could remember was that Lafayette attracts a lot more people, and here, on Liberty, I was free of them. I had my lunch and my independence.

There are few moments more serene than a good summit sit. All around you are views of mountains, streams, waterfalls, forests, and birds, unblemished by human intervention. Such an expanse of nature leaves you in awe, less aware of your thoughts and more aware of the surrounding world. Scanning the landscape from Liberty, my eyes caught sight of a hawk soaring through the mountain valley. Watching it lift elegantly with the wind, its purpose simple and clear, my thoughts flew with it and I was guided towards the singular enjoyment of watching it fly, not curious at all about what it was doing, only hoping to fill my eyes with its movement. As it disappeared over the ridge and my spirit returned to my body, I started thinking of my kids and how I hope they get to experience such things. Love such things. To slow down and feel such things. That in their journey through the rational world, they will personally know these miracles of earth. Because all of it's a miracle. All of it.

Chapter 16

Noobs

Raising four kids is a mess. The TV remote is always lost, nobody can find a matching sock, and dishes pile up so fast it seems that only minutes after I've done them, Liz is doing another load, eyeballing me with an accusatory look that says: *How come I'm the only one who washes dishes around here?* Every day I ask Liz if she's seen my keys or wallet or phone or mind. Every day she says, "No." Mix in driving our kids from one practice to the next, Liz's library trustee meetings, kids I don't even know running through the house during all hours of the day, and tenants calling me twenty-four-seven with their problems, the chaos keeps growing and growing. There are days when Liz and I barely have time to say hello to each other before we go to sleep. And to make life a little crazier, I needed to have some weird mid-life crisis in the middle of all of this, where I disappeared into the mountains at least once every other week, making myself totally unavailable to support the home network. *Yes, yes I did.*

Despite the tumultuous flow of everyday life, nobody on the home front was complaining about my excursions quite yet. My diabolical plan to exercise my mid-life-crisis rights in the wee hours of the morning, during the middle of the week, was paying off. Or perhaps I had an inflated view of my importance and wasn't all that needed at home. Whatever the reason for the continued goodwill at Casa Larson, I let it carry me back to the mountains before anybody could object.

Trying to get out and climb forty-eight large mountains in one year is ludicrous at best, especially for someone new to the gambit. To date, most of the people I met out on the trails had been working on the 4000-footer list for a considerably long time, some even as long as thirty or forty years. In other words, they were an experienced bunch. It made sense, given that all of my ascents involved some level of snow and ice; you'd expect the colder months to draw a hardy crowd. Not only serious climbers, well on their way to completing the forty-eight, but also die-hards doing the list again to complete their "Winter 48," which is when climbers operate under the self-imposed restriction of summiting the 4000-footers exclusively in the winter months. Such activities do not attract a lot of noobs.

But every spring, on one glorious sunny day, New Englanders with no climbing experience at all, emerge from their offices, Cape Cod-style homes, and Colonials, and get the sudden urge to go hiking. Some find local parks in their towns while others crave something bigger. They may have a friend who told them about Lafayette, or a spouse who once climbed it as a kid and promised it would be the greatest thing to do come spring. The warmth of the sun leads them out into their driveways with high hopes and little gear, ready to take on something totally new. For reasons they can't explain, they'll get in their cars and head to Franconia Notch to take on one of the most heralded mountains in New Hampshire climbing lore. And much like my home life, it will be a total mess.

It was on precisely such a day in May that I encountered throngs of these bright-eyed noobs on Mount Lafayette. I wasn't planning on doing either Lafayette or Lincoln this day, but rather the elusive Osceola. Tripoli Road was still closed for the winter, however, so I needed to call another quick audible. I only had a four-hour window before I had to go back and coach my son's baseball game, so there was no time to hesitate. From the Tripoli Road gate I banged a uey and motored up Route 93 to the entrance for Lafayette. I was on a serious mission to get this done, and there would be no lollygagging about. No need to consult Peakbagger, ViewRanger or Google today. I knew exactly where I was going.

Liz and I climbed Lafayette and Lincoln years ago, before we got married, so technically I could have skipped them and claimed mission complete whenever I ended up completing the rest. But for this quest I wanted to bag all forty-eight in one set. Something about skipping ones I had already done years ago felt like cheating. Cheating the accomplishment, but also cheating myself out of the full experience.

With speed on the brain, I ran the first mile up Lafayette and the last mile down Lincoln. For the miles in between, I used my microspikes for most of the way. Having so many 4000-footers under my belt at this point, I felt like a wily old veteran as I sped past baby boomers and college kids. I was also amazed at how many of them were climbing without spikes. By my count there were at least thirty-five noobs slide-stepping and limb-grabbing their way up and down the trails. There were big ones, skinny ones, tall ones, and dumb ones too. Penguins with hands. *What is going on today?*

I started taking account of their footwear. Besides some sensible people with hiking shoes, there were tons of women wearing Keds, a couple men wearing Teva sandals, and one particular imbecile that had elected to climb in flip-flops. On the descent from Lincoln, passing another Ked wearer, it dawned on me that all of these little minnows could use some guidance.

But I can't stand those guys. You know the ones. The know-it-all climbers who think because they have figured out a way that works for them, they have the right to control how others should engage nature. The pyscho Exum guides who believe they are breathing rarified air. Or even worse than them, the Instagram preachers pronouncing that people who aren't true climbers shouldn't bother trying, because they are wrecking the experience for us hardened pros, ya know? Blech. If you want to climb Lafayette and don't know what you're doing, how will you ever learn if you never try?

A lot of the climbers on Lafayette did appear to need help though. Or at least needed to be talked out of climbing up any further. I was moving four times as fast as everybody on the trail, and I didn't have much time to stop and help anybody because I needed to get back for my son's game. *But maybe,* I thought, *I can offer some encouraging words. Or give them something.*

In my pack was an extra pair of Yaktrax and I figured I'd give them to anyone who was willing to take them. Assuming men would be too stubborn and proud to accept any help, I approached older women struggling up the trail while I was on the descent. "Hi," I'd say, "how you doing? Yes, you have a long way to go. Listen, I have an extra set of spikes you can have if you'd like them." *Yes, I know spikes and Yaktrax are not the same thing, but they didn't know that.*

Astonishingly, every woman I offered my Yaktrax to turned them down. They were "good" they said, as they slipped on another chunk of ice and clutched a tree for balance. Each one was quite content to keep plodding along, carrying no supplies, while their husbands trailed behind them with a caring eye, but too far away to help if they actually fell. The first women I tried to help had at least four hours of climbing to go—seven if they were hoping to loop Lafayette in as well. They didn't have a clue what they were doing, but they were determined. Watching them gave me some reassurance that the human spirit is alive and well, if not human intelligence.

After a few more failed attempts at providing help to those who can't be helped, I decided to plunge down the trail at record pace. Now, when another baby boomer made a cute comment about how fast I was going, instead of engaging in conversation and offering them my Yaktrax, I let out a laugh in acknowledgement and replied, "yep," before rambling right on past them. Halfway through my descent I passed a tall graying man with a short ponytail tied off in the back. Probably in his late forties, he looked seasoned, attuned to the ways of the woods—perhaps condescendingly so. He was trying to help out some boomers who were, of course, spikeless. *Good luck, buddy.* Slowing down to eavesdrop on the conversation, I was surprised to hear that these boomers were actually accepting Grayback's help. Grayback was even making a call to his wife, or girlfriend, explaining that he would be home later than expected to help some people get off the mountain. *Good on ya, mate.*

Despite the commotion of the struggling hikers Grayback was helping, scores of hapless individuals continued past them, shuffling their steps and grabbing for trees to avoid slipping and breaking a hip. At the rate they were all going, they wouldn't make summit until nightfall, if at all. I suggested to a few of them that they should go down, given the late hour, but nobody wanted to listen, so on I went. I couldn't understand how nobody could see the peril they were in, but perhaps when everyone around you is making the same mistake, you fail to see it. Every year, people need to be rescued off Lafayette, and today looked like it was going to be a busy one for the New Hampshire Mountain Rescue Service.

A few minutes after passing Grayback, it finally struck me what was transpiring. All of these people, who left their homes in Massachusetts or New Hampshire in seventy- or eighty-degree weather, assumed that after a two-hour drive north to Lafayette, the weather would be the same. They never considered the possibility that a 5000-foot mountain might still have ice on the trails. Or cooler temperatures. Late spring, in my opinion, is the most dangerous time to climb, and I suspect the busiest time for mountain rescue teams. There are way too many people out there who won't accept help, or advice, until the situation is desperate.

Further down the Falling Waters Trail, while contemplating how to join a mountain rescue squad, I came upon the aforementioned young man wearing flip-flops, "leading" his girlfriend up the slope. She was in her early twenties, perhaps in college, and looked athletically capable of any mountain ascent if properly equipped. More athletic than any of the naïve opportunists I had come across earlier, that's for sure. She slipped on some ice as I approached, and when she looked up, caught my concerned glance. "How much longer do we have, do you know?"

"Probably a couple hours, at least."

I looked at her boyfriend, baby-stepping his way up the side of the trail. He reminded me of the obstinate boyfriend from the climb up East Osceola. *Why do these girls date these guys?* After watching him slowly advance a couple of feet, I looked back at the girl who asked me what I thought. "If it was me," I said, "without any spikes, at this late hour, I wouldn't go up. It might be dark by the time you get there, and then you'll have to climb down this at night, which is much more dangerous." She looked back at Flip-flop, who shrugged his shoulders and started upwards again. Well, that was that. "Fuck it," she said, "I'm going down. You can go up if you want to, but this is stupid." Flip-flop started saying, "Whoa, whoa, whoa," but it didn't matter, she was leaving. *There's hope for this one!* I congratulated myself for possibly ending another bad relationship in the Whites and locating at least one person who still had brains. The human race might survive after all.

Chapter 17

Hunted

Halfway up the Mount Willey Trail I could feel someone watching me, no, *hunting me.* Somewhere out there was a cunning predator that I could hear but couldn't see. Every thirty paces or so, a sound like a tiny engine sputtering would start up, only to come to an abrupt halt whenever I turned around to catch the stalker in the act. *Who are you?*

I started timing the beating of wings according to my steps. *One, two . . . nine, ten—ten!* Without fail, every ten steps after the flapping started, it stopped. *Aha! I have you now.* Feeling very clever, I devised a plan to turn around on the fifth step. I'd make him think all was normal and then WHAMO! Caught in the snide! Cue the evil laugh. *Heh, heh, heh.* I started walking again and on step five, twisted my head around and saw a pair of wings darting twenty feet above my head. No wonder I couldn't see him before. He zipped up to the nearest branch, hoping to avoid detection, but it was too late. *Gotchya!*

It was no surprise to discover that a gray jay was my pursuer. I had a sneaking suspicion, given my previous run-ins with them on Mount Tom. Tom was, after all, right next to Willey. Additionally, the internet was abound with stories of gray jay sightings on Willey. People were even known to feed them right out of their hands. Before I even got out of my car that morning, I decided if there was ever a chance to feed a jay, today would be the day.

Keeping a consistent distance of about ten feet behind and twenty feet above, my little shadow trailed me for the next hour, determined to see what I was carrying. Grabbing some granola from my pack, I displayed it on my hand and offered it up. "Here you go, want some?" Five minutes passed while I stood in the middle of the trail with my hand out, staring at this bird cocking his head back and forth. Hoping to lure him in, I set the granola chunks on some rocks and continued up the path. With a little more distance between us, he divebombed his quarry, scarfed it down, and proceeded to follow me another two thousand feet up the trail.

At the summit was a small clearing where he had no choice but to hop close if he wanted to see what I was about. Unfortunately for him, a few other jays showed up and the odds tipped in my favor. If they were going to get my food, they were going to have to fight for it. This time when I presented another nugget of granola, it was only seconds before a gray jay fluttered down and picked my hand clean. I couldn't believe it. *Holy crow, this works?*

I grabbed some more granola and held my hand out again. Another jay, or at least I think it was a different jay, flew down and grabbed the spoils. This was too much fun. I was giggly. What lunacy was coming over me that the act of feeding a couple of birds could turn me into the equivalent of a child scoring Halloween candy? How could something so simple, so easy, feel so magical? *Thank you, Mr. Willey, thank you.*

Their bellies full, the little gluttons abandoned me as I got up and ventured my way over to the summit of Field to grab my second 4000-footer of the day. It didn't take too long. But despite the quick conquer, and Field marking the twentieth mountain on the list for me, I didn't feel much like celebrating; I was ready to get out of there. Field was pleasant, but I must admit, I preferred Willey. Willey had better views of Crawford Notch, and of course, more interactive entertainment. Or maybe I was simply bonking too much to enjoy Field because I had given away all my granola and was still very hungry. Steering my mind from my exhaustion, I went on autopilot and thundered down the trail for home.

My thoughts returned when I reached the trailhead where my car was parked, and I was suddenly struck by a notion that came completely out of the blue: *Will this be the mountain that wrecks my marriage? Whoa, where did that come from?* There was nothing wrong with my marriage; Liz and I were doing great. But I do get nervous sometimes, especially in the early morning hours when I'm driving away to another mountain and leaving her with the kids to deal with. I can't help but occasionally wonder, *Am I pushing my luck?* I'm quite confident that I'll be climbing these mountains well into my sixties, and will probably climb all of the 4000-footers again then, so really, what's the rush?

As forty drew closer, more and more people I knew were getting divorced or having an affair, women and men alike. Neither sex was better. Everybody shares the blame. With all of the bad relationship stuff happening around us, I couldn't help but wonder if I was going to upset the marital balance in my life with this hare-brained adventure I was on. Liz is so agreeable about everything that of course she says, "No, no, no, go ahead and do it." But I always have this guilt when I'm doing something for myself that it's going to turn people away from me. That they'll feel like I'm letting them down. It's probably a Massachusetts Catholic thing, implanted in my youth, guilty just for being alive.

Guilt is a funny thing. It can make you act better than you really are but also limit you from living out your best life. It can lead you to make some good life choices but imprison you with a lifetime of worry about how you make others feel. The first half of my life was consumed with guilt for no reason at all. It's an awful feeling and I hope my kids know that they don't need to live a life ridden with it. That has been my issue; I don't want it to be theirs.

My guilt makes me move fast. I've always had this feeling that if I can move faster than everybody else, they won't notice when I'm not around to help. That if I get up a little earlier than everyone, work a little harder than everyone, a little faster, I can be well on my way to having more money and a better life, without seeming selfish to the people I care about. I move like my time doesn't belong to me, but everyone else, and that the only way to get "me time" is to do it when nobody is looking. It's a problem, I know. I'm working on it.

Even if they don't have the same guilt issues as me, as people get over the hill, they still worry about whether they are moving fast enough. They figure if they can have more fun than anybody else, do more things than anybody else, they will have a bigger life tally and therefore have a more worthwhile life. I'm not ashamed to say that climbing the 4000-footers falls right into that. Taking on these mountains certainly had something to do with adding an accomplishment to my life tally, and I was excited to think about finishing something only a few thousand people had ever done in the past.

But after hiking Field, driving home from another land conquered, I noted that the tally didn't mean that much to me anymore. Twenty mountains felt like a good enough dent for me and anyone else who cared. Besides, it's not like completing the 4000-footer list is the end-all and be-all of mountain accomplishments—not even by New England standards. There are always more lists to tackle. The Appalachian Mountain Club (AMC) offers certificates for completing these same forty-eight in winter, as well as for doing all sixty-seven of the 4000-footers in New England. There's also the one-hundred highest in New England list, which includes the 4000-footers plus a bunch of 3000-footers. Once you're done with those, you can do the grid and climb all of the forty-eight in every month of the year. If that doesn't do it for you, and you're still lacking for entertainment, you can redline every trail in the state, where summits aren't the goal—simply hiking every marked trail on the map is. After that, you can do the forty-eight all over again, but this time backwards, naked, and covered in honey to see how many bears you can outrun.

The lists never end, so why does it even matter if I complete the list at all? It's simple, really: quitting is a hard habit to break. I always want to be the kind of person that says what he means, and means what he says, and I said I'd climb all of these mountains before I hit forty, dammit. If I didn't, I'd feel guilty about that too. So, rather than deal with whatever causes me to feel guilty over inconsequential matters, I decided that the only way to relieve said guilt, and any pressure this adventure may start causing at home, was to work faster on the list.

Chapter 18

Climbing Fast

It was May and the Mount Osceola Trail was precariously slick from the rapid snow melt. Imbalanced slabs of schist and granite, pitched at sharp angles, littered the path, making it incredibly difficult to get proper footing. Even if I was hiking at a leisurely pace, it would have been tricky to keep my feet, but I was angry at this mountain, so I was running it. Three times I planned on ascending Osceola, and three times my plans had been foiled: once for lack of proper gear and twice for misjudging when the Tripoli Road access would finally open. Osceola needed to pay. *Okay, are we losing our grip here Matt?*

For the ascent I didn't carry a pack—only a water belt—and managed to make the 3.2-mile climb to the summit in an hour's time. This was remarkable for me. To be clear, I am not a runner and I am not a hard-core athlete. I like to participate in 5Ks and some snowshoe races now and again, but I'm satisfied if I can get out there and beat a few of the guys that are ten years older than me. I'm in it for the experience, not the glory. But on this day, I crushed Osceola like a bug. An hour after summiting, I was back in the car and on my way home.

My destruction of Osceola marked my fastest ascent of any mountain on the 4000-footer list. Leaving my pack in the truck certainly helped, as did putting away the smartphone. There was no time for taking pictures today. No pausing to look around and record any musings about nature and society. No. Today was about one thing and one thing only: REVENGE! Osceola was in my way and needed to be dealt with swiftly and in an unceremonious fashion. And yet, despite my speed, I remember everything about this climb. I was a hurricane on Osceola and can still recall, several years later, the way the rocks felt on my feet, the faces I met, the view from the summit, and the way the sun warmed my face. My previous ascents reminded me of the importance of slowing down, and how doing so enables you to be more present, but Osceola showed me that being present is possible while moving fast, as long as you eliminate your distractions and focus fully on the moment. Because I was present, I can replay the memories of that hurried day in slow motion.

Never before, and never since, have I run up and down a mountain as sizeable as this, from start to finish. En route to the summit, I passed a family who was in awe of the speed with which I was moving. The wife said, "Oh my goodness," as her poor husband lugged their two-year-old on his back. When I passed them again on the way down, the wife was shocked. "Didn't we just see you pass us on the way up?" *Yes, ma'am. Yes, you did.* I guess I was getting in pretty good shape, though pictures from my kid's little league game that evening told a different story. Better than a few months before, but definitely still not trim. And of course, there was no amount of climbing that could turn the clock back on my graying hair.

I'm not going to lie; gray hairs took me a little while to get over. They started popping up on my face a few years back and even though growing a strong goatee wasn't on my wish list, losing the chance to grow a youthful one sent me into a panic. *Oh my God, am I getting old?* Then I panicked that I was panicking and thought, *Oh my God, did I just make myself grow older because I panicked about my gray hairs?* STOP PANICKING! *I can't!* YOU HAVE TO! *I know!* But the grays in my beard I could shave. Easy fix. When they first appeared above my temples, it was a different story.

At first, I decided to try covering them up with *Just for Men* hair dye. Some months I'd do it, some I wouldn't, so my "look" pinballed between seasoned office manager and aging baseball player. After a few tries, I gave it up. Wearing plastic gloves and rubbing paint on my scalp was a vanity commitment I wasn't ready to make. I also didn't feel like I was being me anymore, worrying about my hair. Maybe it was because it was the more convenient option, but I eventually decided that I wanted my children to have an honest understanding of their father, and aging, so I threw the rest of my *Just for Men* products out a few weeks before Osceola, resolved to never bother with it again. Who knew that *Just For Men* could lead to such existential self-evaluation?

Being comfortable in your own skin, gray hairs or not, is paramount for living your best life. Hands down. No contest. If you can love yourself, all that follows is easier. I usually don't have any problem with this, but gray hairs take a little adjustment because they appear before you think they should. One day you're climbing up and down a mountain like you're twenty-five and the next day you're standing in front of the mirror shaving, catching silver flickers out of the corner of your eye—signs of a demise you have no control over. It's the lack of control that's terrifying.

I can get myself comfortable with the idea that I am going to die at some point; what gets me squirrely in my seat is knowing that it won't be on my own terms. That I don't get a say in when it happens, nor the circumstance. Mortality, I accept, but maybe a thousand years from now. Not sixty or less. Sheesh. There are some who like to claim that they are above all of this, and that "age is just a number," but I think they are only saying this to trick themselves. Nobody wants to see gray hairs in the mirror, and nobody wants to feel sore after laying down for a night in bed. One of the cruelest realities of getting older is that our bodies feel worse from a night in bed, resting, than they do going for a walk or a run. How does that even make sense?

Ah well. Whaddya gonna do? Better not to look back on what's lost or try to grasp it again as if the gray hairs aren't there. It took a whole lot of mountains to get there, but I started realizing that the grays are a gift, sent to remind me that I have other things to do. More important things. A long time ago I decided that the only healthy way to live is to feel like today is the best day of your life, and that everything going forward is going to be better than today. This year is going to be better than last year, next year better than this one, and so on. No looking back, no regrets. It was time to apply that logic again, no longer worrying about aging, but accepting it, even embracing it, as part of the equation for experiencing an ever-improving life. A life that is gaining importance, not losing it, with every year earned.

Our lives are like the expanding universe, constantly growing and extending into new territory. As we grow and build relationships, make friendships, live and work, marry, have children, and someday hopefully become grandparents, our actions send ripples into the world that are not only felt by the people we directly meet and love, but countless others who we will never even know about. So the question becomes, are you a help or a hurt? Like the chicken scratches that winter climbers leave behind on the rocky paths with their spikes, the marks we leave behind aren't always seen, but always there, waiting for the spring ice melt. When they do reveal themselves, will they have a positive or negative effect?

In the end we all die, and barring some exceptional cases, most of us, and our work, will be forgotten. The only way we are truly remembered then is not by our names, but through the positive output of our lives, because that energy transfers to the people around you, allowing your energy to live on. If you are a good dad, your kids will remember that and share what they've learned with their kids. If you are a good friend, your friends will be better friends to others, and your positivity perpetuates itself.

When I leave this life, I want it to be with as many positive feelings as possible, because in the end, that is the great aggregate; that is the great accumulation of wealth that one can ever hope to achieve. Not how many points you scored against others, but how many points you helped others score. That's the only tally that matters. If the good you've done outshines the bad, then you have led a life worth living. Simple as that. If you don't have a sense of which way your scale is tipping though, it's time to figure it out and act, because gray hairs come faster than you think.

Chapter 19

A Pile of Rocks

Not many people know this, but the Anglo-Saxon sounding name of Hale is actually an old Native American word pronounced "Hal-ay," meaning "boring mountain that needs a mighty cairn at the summit to make it more interesting." Okay, fine. Hale is in fact an English name meaning "nook" or "retreat," but that has nothing to do with this mountain either. It was actually named for Reverend Edward Everett Hale, who lobbied for a forestation program in the area during his time as chaplain of the United States Senate. Given the appearance of this mountain, I'm not sure the Senate thought much of his efforts.

Rain was in the forecast, making motivation difficult. Thunder and lightning were scheduled as well. A beautiful sunrise welcomed the day and momentarily deceived me into thinking the weatherman might be customarily wrong, but as I rounded the bend past Exit 23 on Route 93, the sky turned bleak. I didn't want to climb today, but the night before I had seen a Jack Kerouac quote on Instagram that read, "You'll never remember the lawns that you mowed and the time spent taking care of your yard, so go climb the goddamn mountain." Social media is so inspiring.

On a dismal, rainy day, the Hale Brook Trail is a little creepy at best. The trail felt shrouded, with trees closing in all around me; signs that the summer growth was amping up. It made me feel hot and claustrophobic. Ten minutes into the hike I took my rain jacket off, despite the steady drizzle.

This was the first mountain where I was hiking in the same old hiking pants I used on Kilimanjaro, some twenty-two years ago. Contrary to what others would suggest, I do not still own the pants because I'm an old yank who never throws anything out. I actually love throwing stuff away. It's one of my favorite hobbies. Getting rid of the crap in my house is how I spend fifty percent of my free time. But I have a hard time parting with anything connected to that Kilimanjaro climb. Plus, the pants still worked great—why get rid of them? The EMS backpack I was using also came from the Kilimanjaro trip. *Ah, they used to build things that lasted in this country.*

I love having this gear that connects me to where my relationship with mountains began. They are simple reminders that all you really need in order to go anywhere in this world are some reliable pants and a good pack. And a shirt, I guess. Sure, there are all of these great new technologies nowadays, and it's cool that I can record voice notes off my smartphone and use a GPS app to locate my position on almost any trail. But you don't need those things in order to depend on yourself in the wilderness, so long as you make a good plan and take note of where you're at. Some snacks, an extra layer of clothing, water, and paying attention to your surroundings, pretty much covers it. Having a few simple things on the trail can sufficiently take care of you as long as you are mindful about how to take care of them.

I'd like to tell you that climbing Hale conjured up all of the wonderful feelings most of my other hikes did, with a deep love of nature and gratefulness about the opportunity to experience such things, but I'd be lying. Climbing Hale sucked. The trail was drenched, the mountain was ugly, and my only reward when I made it to the top was a giant pile of rocks, presumably stacked there over the years by other climbers who were disappointed in the lack of natural aesthetics. I found myself looking forward to getting back to work. Yep, Hale was that bland. I started cursing the list. *Why have a list that includes this stupid mountain?* Supposedly you can snag a tiny view of the surrounding mountains if you climb the cairn and look out over the trees, but all I saw was gray.

Making things worse, I really had to go. I'm not much of one for talking about bowel movements or bodily fluids of any kind, but one of the biggest drawbacks to doing these climbs in the early morning is that I always have "to go" right around the time I summit. Climbing would be far more pleasant if I could start in the afternoon, after my morning constitutional. Most times it's not a big deal, but on Hale I was downright uncomfortable.

It was too bad I couldn't combine Hale with some other mountains, because Hale didn't deserve the special treatment of being climbed in isolation. Maybe there are other days where Hale looks better and offers a more enjoyable climb, but Hale was the first peak on the list that I would not bother coming back to, and would never bother with at all, unless it appeared on the 4000-footer list. Hey, they can't all be winners. No point ruminating about it. Better just to pick up and move on.

Chapter 20

Alone in the Dark

The trail was socked in. For the first two hours I didn't see anybody, and it was a downright lonely climb. I broke trail in the afternoon and the constant cloud cover foretold that night would descend earlier than usual. *Am I going to have to climb down in the dark?* To comfort myself from that thought, I started singing some gibberish that originated from nowhere but my head, off the cuff: *You gotta put one foot fo' the other, try to help your brother, and plow on for the reasons, the reasons that you say. And I bluhhhh* (trying to keep the song going, can't think of words) *the money and the time and everyone knows it's all been rügggh . . . No, no. no. That's no good.* While searching for better words, the winds started howling, arriving just in time to help me complete my song. *They say that everything you hear, is what you fear, so everybody hold on, it's gonna be a windy one tonight.* Yikes.

My lyrical prose was only slightly less scary than the weather. The winds picked up another notch as I reached the higher elevations, and the pine trees fluttered back and forth like fingers drumming a desk. As I neared the summit, I tried to spot some glimmer of the surrounding mountains, but it was no use; the sky was a screen of gray film blanketing everywhere I looked. Voices lifted from somewhere off trail, maybe forty yards below me. I could make out laughter, but somehow it wasn't inviting. The sounds of chatter emerging through the dank forest reminded me of gangsters in a Western movie, hiding out in the desert hills.

I came upon a spar trail leading to the Garfield Ridge Campsite, which was about two-tenths of a mile below where I was. *That's where the voices must be coming from. Somebody is camping up here tonight?* I heard a woman conversing with a man, and it sounded like they were camping separately. What a way to meet someone for the first time. It made me sympathetic about what it must feel like to be a woman, alone in a tent, camped on a mountain slope with nothing but fog, rain, and a stranger to keep you company. I've read too many stories, but I'd be sleeping with a knife under my pillow. *And I'm a dude!*

No wonder so many single women hikers climb with big menacing dogs. I'm always bumping into athletic women in their twenties, bounding up and down the trails, accompanied by a Boxer, a German Shepherd, or some wolf-dragon-demon that looks like it has sized me up as its next meal. I'm glad women find comfort in having these beasts with them, but if their goal is to totally turn the tables on thousands of years of fear at the hands of men, well they have succeeded. I'm terrified when I see them coming my way.

When I arrived at the summit, it was so blustery, I wished that I had long hair and a YouTube channel; the conditions were perfect for ripping some air guitar while seeing if I could keep my balance facing the wind. When I stood atop the large concrete block situated at the summit, a strong gust blew me back, and I sat down for fear of being swept off the mountain. It made me think of all those videos you see of people battling winds on the summit of Mt. Washington. The moment called for a rare selfie. Making sure to get the Tesla rock band T-shirt I was wearing in the frame, I snapped a photo and sent it to my buddy Steve, who shared my affinity for Tesla and is a kind enough friend that he would actually care I was hanging out on a mountaintop in a windstorm like the psychopath that I am. He replied, "Be careful."

Twenty minutes into my descent, I was enveloped by the night. This was my first time alone on a mountain in the dark, and the experience was both exhilarating and nerve-wracking. What would I encounter? Bears? The previous year I bought my dad one of those wilderness cameras you attach to a tree for taking wildlife photos. Knowing absolutely nothing about bears' eating, sleeping, or moving habits, I found an overturned tree in the woods, brimming with termites, and positioned the camera fifteen feet away from it. That was at 6:30pm.

At 7:30pm, a mama bear and her cub sauntered through the exact spot I had been an hour before, clambering right over the fallen tree. When I retrieved the camera the next day and reviewed the footage, I couldn't believe I had been that close to a bear without even knowing it. And it was a mama and her cub! The images freaked me out a little because I had heard that mama bears were the most dangerous to run into, especially if they thought you were too close to their cubs.

Now the mama bear and her cub came back to me, and my antenna went up. Thinking of bears got me thinking about other animals who go bump in the night, like wolves. *Wolves!* Wolves got me thinking about mountain lions. *Mountain lions! Lions, Tigers, and Bears, Oh My!* It was time to make some noise. I went into the music library on my phone and clicked "play all" on every Tesla song I had, turning the volume up all the way. Then with headlamp on, I moved out at a slight trot, singing as loudly as I could. No man nor beast for twenty miles would escape my off-key bellowing. Not if I could help it. I was NOT going to be eaten in the dark!

Thankfully, I was not eaten in the dark. When I finally got back to my truck, I had to laugh at myself. *What a maroon. Bears?* Bears know you are there well before you do, and as long as you make a little noise, will stay far clear of you. I was making enough racket to wake the dead and send bears running for the ocean. Bears would not be a problem.

Mountain lions? There are always rumors of mountain lions creeping back into the New Hampshire forests. The chances of me running into a mountain lion were as good as being struck by lightning, right? Still, making a little noise and wearing a headlamp couldn't hurt. To a mountain lion I would appear to be a menacing, deranged alien, capable of unleashing dangerous claws and a venomous attack, right? Okay, not worried about mountain lions.

Wolves? A few years back I ran into a wolf in my parents' yard one night. My parents were away on vacation, and I was pranking them by putting the leg lamp from *A Christmas Story* in their front window for all the neighbors to see. It was huge. The wolf, not the leg lamp. The size of it startled me.

Growing up we always had coyotes in the area, a couple of which once ate my mom's tiny dogs: a Yorkshire terrier named Pretzel and a Maltese named Puff Ball. I mean, can you blame the coyotes? Pretzel and Puff Ball sounded delicious. When I got home from school on the day of the murders, my mom was in a panic, and promptly sent me to the backyard to go after the coyotes and rescue her small dogs. Unfortunately, a thorough inspection revealed nothing but some white tufts of fur left behind on the grass, all that remained of poor Puff Ball. Lying in bed that night, reflecting upon the carnage, it occurred to me that my mom hadn't hesitated to literally throw me *at* the wolves.

But those were skinny coyotes that were skittish around humans. This thing near my parents' driveway was different. I did some research and discovered that crossbreeding of wolves and coyotes had resulted in the emergence of a new animal in New England over the last several years: the coywolf. What I saw in my parents' yard that night wasn't a wolf, but a coywolf. I remembered how it stared right back at me and didn't scurry away like the coyotes of my youth. Its casual confidence was chilling. Could there be coywolves out there in the woods with me as I ramble about the White Mountains?

Over the years I've had all sorts of strange animal encounters: the wild boar that charged me in the forests of Alabama, the unseen growl I ran away from at Moosehead Lake in Maine, the racoons that crept up on my feet in the middle of the night while camping in my backyard, the red squirrel that attacked me in my basement. You'll forgive me if life has left me not so trusting of our furry friends. Is it so ludicrous to think a coywolf could attack me? A better question is, why hadn't I brought anything to protect myself? I have no doubt that the scariest thing in the woods was probably not an animal but a middle-aged man singing Tesla songs with a light beam shooting from his head, but shouldn't I have a little protection? During the descent of Garfield, I pondered all of the weapons I could have brought from home: a knife, an axe, a ping pong paddle. *Anything would have been better than this!* Having no other defense, I sang as loudly as possible, and fortunately, all dangers, real or imagined, disappeared. I've needed no other strategy since.

Chapter 21

A Moose in the Path

Witnessing a summit sunset was on my mind. I also had two extremely challenging climbs coming up over the Presidentials and the Carter Range, both of which exceeded twenty miles, so I needed some longer training climbs to prepare for those experiences. I found a fourteen-mile trek that would take me over North and South Twin, as well as Galehead, and realized there was a fair chance that if I went for them all at once, I would likely have to descend under the cover of night. I wasn't looking forward to feeling like a scared jackrabbit again, but if I was going to get stuck in the deep, dark woods, I figured I may as well embrace it and get to watch the sun go down over the mountains.

Before heading out, there wasn't much information I could find to ascertain what the North Twin Trail was like, but what I discovered was beautiful. Along the side of the trail runs a little river called, well, Little River, and after a mile it converged with the trail in what was to be the first of three river crossings. The first crossing went okay, but on the second one, I couldn't find a clear rock bridge to help me get across. In retrospect, I should have taken my socks and shoes off and waded through, but there was a rock in the middle of the river, hidden an inch below the water's surface, beckoning me. Convinced that I could hit it with a quick toe-tap, hop onto another partially submerged rock with a second toe-tap, and then jump to safety on the other side, I launched myself into action. It was a foolish plan. On the second toe-tap, my right foot plunged into the river, completely soaking my boot and two layers of socks. To keep my left foot from getting wet as well, I hopped across the rest of the river on one leg. *Only twelve miles to go. Great.*

When I reached the next river crossing, you'd think I'd learn, but no—I tried to tap dance my way across again, only to have my right foot plunge into the water—again. Now completely drenched, there was no doubt my foot was going to pay a heavy price. On the other side of the river, I sat down to remove my boot and wring out my socks. I was actually wearing two types: Lofoten and Smartwool, hoping the combination would wick away sweat and prevent blisters. I never planned on wicking away river water.

The soggy foot was a problem, but by the time I hit the summit of South Twin, it wasn't as bad as I expected, so I continued with my plan to tackle Galehead. I needed to move though. Sunset began as I passed the Galehead hut, casting honey-yellow light across the treetops of the valley below. I wanted to linger and absorb the view, but there wasn't any time: I still needed to backtrack up and over the Twins, and I didn't want to do so in the dark. Determined, but exhausted, one thought repeated itself as I made my second ascent of South Twin: *Hodor, Hodor, Hodor*—a consequence of having watched too much *Game of Thrones*.

But my efforts were rewarded when I finally returned to North Twin's summit, for there I got to take in the greatest sunset I think I've ever seen. Orange and purple hues clasped the surrounding mountains, comforting the earth below me like a swaddled baby. Everything looked so cozy and warm despite the dropping temperature. I've seen some great sunsets before: eye-popping ones over the Golden Gate Bridge from the rooftop of my apartment building, glorious ones from the cliff edge of the Grand Canyon, but this one, from the top of North Twin, had me in rapture. I suspect that was mainly because I earned it. Unable to pull myself from snapping photos until the sun disappeared from the earth, I waited until nightfall to ready myself for the long descent.

Four miles doesn't sound like a far way to go in the dark alone, but it sure felt it. By now I had completely abandoned any fear of mountain lions or bears, and single coywolves gave me no concern. *But what if there were three or four of those things tracking me, waiting to pounce?* With no cell service to tap into and blast my entire music library for the coywolves, I was stuck having to sing away my fears without any accompaniment. *The humanity! Lewis and Clark never had it so bad.* All sorts of weirdness came out of my mouth as I stomped my way down, hitting trees with my hiking poles, and fording the rivers.

When I met the river crossings again, I successfully navigated the first one without getting wet, but on the second and third crossings, I had no choice but to wade in. Holding my phone as a flashlight in one hand while holding my hiking poles in the other, made hopping on rocks too dangerous to attempt. So I plunged into the river, shouting a number of expletives and war cries to carry me to the other side. Delirium was setting in and I'm not entirely sure what I said, but what I do remember, I found inappropriate for even my own ears. I must have gone Berserker, because plowing through the river made me feel like a crazed Viking warrior.

When I got back to my car, I was buzzing from having completed the wildest hike yet: seven hours over five mountains, battling darkness, rivers, and blisters. After fourteen miles on the trail, eating the Italian sub I saved for the drive home was pure bliss. The only thing that would have made the meal more divine was a glass of milk. I never wanted a glass of milk so much in my entire life. Maybe it was the hot peppers, but water wasn't cutting it, so I prayed to God to make an all-night "packy" store appear. The seriousness of my prayer made me laugh. It also got me thinking I should probably spend a little more time thanking God for giving me the opportunity to do this, even if He didn't make a convenience store appear.

God has become a tricky subject lately, hasn't it? It feels like nowadays you can't even confess your belief in God without risking offending someone. As such, I would now like to apologize to anyone out there who thought this was simply going to be a nature-lover book, devoid of any mention of God. I admit it, I think there's a God. But please hear me out, before you toss this book out the window.

Look, I don't care if you believe in God or not. But no matter what your religion (or lack of one) is, I think we can all agree that something magical, and still beyond explanation, has occurred here to create an extraordinary opportunity to explore this strange universe together. We have been given a tremendous gift, whether by random chance, or celestial beings. I choose to believe there is a special power. Call it energy, call it God, call it whatever you want.

I'm not a Bible-thumper—heck, I can only manage to get my family to go to church on Christmas and Easter. But even if you subscribe to the Big Bang Theory, let me suggest another beginning. Whether you argue that first there was nothing, or a host of elements exploding that created the universe as we know it today, something had to come before either scenario to provide the conditions that made the Big Bang possible. Nothing is still something, and those "chemical" reactions didn't spontaneously generate themselves—something had to produce them and the conditions for them to interact, even if it was merely another set of chemicals and elements. Through this logic, it's clear to me that any beginning has to be the result of some other creation that preceded it, and on and on it goes, backwards through time. A perpetual, infinite cycle of creation. The only word I can fathom to encapsulate that is "God."

When I was a teenager, I remember a few moments when I swore that I could feel God around me. Those moments always came when I was out in nature. Perhaps they were endorphins. Perhaps it was spiked serotonin. But I wasn't vigorously exercising or playing anything. I was simply walking along on a beautiful day when every part of me felt warmed by a presence I could not identify. I felt connected to everything around me, like I had the force.

Climbing these mountains was stirring those feelings again, making me feel more connected, reminding me that much like the cells that make up my body, I am but one cell in the developing human spirit. That for too long I'd been stuck in my own story, caring about the wrong things. Still cared too much about what other people wanted from me. Still cared if I got invited to cocktail parties because I told funny stories. Still cared that people respected my career. Still cared that I looked young and fit.

We all have a tendency to live in our own story; not just our own head, but our own story. How often does a friend or family member tell you the same story? How many times do you rehash the same story for them? Maybe we are all losing our memory bit by bit, but I think what is really going on is that we live so much in our own story, we forget who we have told what to already. The noise of regular life has us so desperately seeking our own legitimate worth in the human context, that we often focus too singularly on our own human development to the neglect of others. As a result, when we aren't ruminating about our own story, we are seeking an audience to validate its significance. Like some writer penning a memoir.

But something was happening to me now. Facing forty was like stumbling upon a moose on the trail. There you are, walking along a path you've been quite happily walking for years, when suddenly you turn a corner and are met by something scary. Liz and I once bumped into a moose while hiking Paintbrush Canyon in the Tetons. We were talking and laughing, obliviously moving along, when we almost ran into a mama moose as we rounded a hook in the thickly wooded trail. Instinctively, we leapt behind some trees and waited, both excited and nervous about what could happen next. It brought forth all sorts of questions: How do we get by it? What if it's protecting its calf? Would it charge? Do moose charge? Has anybody ever been killed by a moose?

Fortunately, after fifteen minutes or so, the moose headed off the trail towards a couple of other moose and we were free to proceed. But running smack into one gave us pause and made us recognize that we were not alone. Forty is like that. All the little adventures and accomplishments you have had to date suddenly seem so insignificant, and it makes you reflect upon the choices you've made and the choices you'll make next. It makes you wonder: *Have I been on the right path? Have I been living the right story?*

When I was growing up, more than anything else, I wanted to be a writer. My dad always laughed about it, telling me I better be prepared to be broke. I never quite believed him until a few years ago when I took up a side gig writing for an online legal journal focused on real estate transactions. The most I ever made was $100 per article—not a good return for several hours of work. Worse, after submitting my pieces, the editors would alter them with grammatically incorrect wording, forcing me to re-edit their edits before publication. It wasn't worth the effort.

In high school there was one class I was especially excited to take: Creative Writing. This was partly because it was a writing class, but mostly because it was the only opportunity we had to actually "create" something. Since the education system decided woodshop was no longer important, Creative Writing was going to be my chance to build! To make things happen! To show the world that we men weren't all that bad, you know? My writing style focused primarily on dialogue and character development, and it turned out, was the least popular of the submitted pieces. The "best" pieces, according to my teacher, were the ones that used words like marigold and ubiquitous, and would spend an entire page describing exactly what a chair looked like, how it felt to sit in that chair, and how sitting in that chair made one think of their grandmother and their grandmother's hands, followed by two pages of how the grandmother's wrinkled hands marked the passages of time, reflecting a life of beauty and strife and fire. It was awful.

I wanted to write something real. My favorite movie of all time then, and still today, is *Midnight Run*. If you're not familiar with it, it stars Robert DeNiro and Charles Grodin, two polar-opposite personalities stuck together on a cross-country trip of epic failures. Grodin's character, "The

Duke," laundered money from the mob and is considered a white-collar criminal who skipped bail, and DeNiro plays the bounty hunter sent to bring him back to jail. The dialogue is laced with profanities, anger, humor, and the heartfelt realism of two good, but very different men. I wanted to write stories like that.

So I wrote about men and boys and girls, working through real life scenarios. I wrote about first jobs and teenage discussions on figuring out life. I made jokes about high-collared shirts and convertible Mercedes, ubiquitously present at stuffy private schools like the one I was attending. I proffered that there has to be more to life than trying to become rich or an academic adored for their ability to speak in non-literal terms. Boy, did I choose the wrong audience. My teacher told me to come up with more descriptive elements, foregoing dialogue and real-world scenarios, until I wrote some crap about the red and green lights of a traffic light as a symbolic reference to a man's life rolling down a major byway; it was halting, I said. I don't remember much of it except that I hated writing it, and my teacher considered it an acceptable "piece," worthy of publication in the student rag. The experience convinced me that if the things I like writing about aren't worthy of publication, I shouldn't bother. What a mistake that was.

In college, my mom, knowing the world was pushing me away from writing, suggested I go into journalism, but I hate that kind of writing. I don't want to be on the beat, pestering people, and I'm not looking to uproot someone's life story, whatever the cost. When I was eighteen, a friend who worked for *The Globe* tried to get some dirt from me on another friend connected to a story he was about to break. It horrified me that he would try to take advantage of my friendship to get the scoop. No, journalism wasn't for me. I wanted to write books, but didn't want to be broke either, so I put off writing and picked up the mantle of real-life responsibilities, completely shelving my dream.

I majored in business and information systems, which I don't regret. If your parents are going to pay for a college education, you better make damn sure it's going to pay off financially. The investment is too big, especially nowadays. What kept me motivated for a life without writing was the fear of a life without a family. I already loved my unborn children so much that it was a no-brainer to pursue a degree in subjects I wasn't currently interested in, all so that I could support them when they were born. Looking back though, it's too bad I didn't minor in English and drop one of the business degrees; my college forgot to note one of my majors on my final transcript anyway. Typical.

But my kids are here now, and I've been able to support them with a good life. At least I think so. So, what now? What's next? Despite the fear that life is half over, there is something very freeing about turning forty. With each year that passes, I worry less about offending people or what people will think of me. In my youth I worried that my writing wouldn't be unique enough to warrant the words and would somehow fall short of other's expectations. What I should have concerned myself with was my own expectations.

If I never climbed these mountains or started writing about them, nobody would think any less of me, but I would know that I didn't pursue a dream, and in my mind, I would be a failure. I can't live with that. How can I ever tell my kids to pursue their dreams if I never do it myself? For the first half of my life, I was chicken to do this, either due to bad advice or misinterpretation, or perhaps for fear that I would lose a piece of me by opening myself up to the world. One of the blessings about turning forty is that it makes you realize time is short, and since you can't hold onto your life forever, you may as well share as much as you can, while you can.

Chapter 22

#Instagame

The day after watching the sunset on the Twins, I took my daughter Chloe out of school for something far more important than class time: father-daughter time on Mount Monadnock. She was only eight, but my climbing had caught her attention, and she expressed an interest in tackling her own mountain. The morning of, I let her go to school as if it was another normal day, and then surprised her with an early dismissal thirty minutes later. She was so excited.

At 3,150 feet, Monadnock doesn't quite compare to any of the 4000-footers, but it's still a legit hike and a mighty long one for an eight-year-old kid. Or so I thought. Chloe bounded up the Dublin Trail with tremendous energy, only needing a couple of breaks. Encountering few hikers and plenty of mosquitoes along the way, the ascent lulled me into believing the false promise of an unoccupied summit. I figured that since school wasn't out yet, we were certain to have Monadnock to ourselves. I was dead wrong.

Scores of teenagers on school trips littered the summit, along with baby boomers in Patagonia clothing and several young families. Hard-pressed to find a quiet spot to enjoy our hard-earned lunch, we scooted down the mountain fifty yards to a nice bald spot that appeared to be fairly out of the way from the masses. But as we settled onto our perch, the air was filled with boisterous chatter about selfies and "instagame."

Ten college-aged women appeared, decked out in a variety of pink and black spandex. There were around one hundred and fifty people spread out over the expanse of Monadnock's summit, but all you could hear were these young women. Upon arrival, one of them busted out a six-foot-tall selfie stick and choreographed a nine-person yoga shot, with all of her subjects doing a crow pose. The entire summit was riveted by the display.

Dissatisfied with her original composition, Selfie-stick instructed one crow to get up and move to another spot for artistic purposes. She then advised another girl who was distraught, because crow proved to be too difficult for her. Selfie-stick put her arm around Can't-Do-Crow, said some reassuring words, and made her and another girl do some sort of tree pose at either end of the crows in order to help frame out the shot. The visual now perfectly sculpted, she snapped the shot and genuinely praised the girls on how their "instagame just went up." It was like watching some strange alien support group.

Up until this moment I'd been loving Instagram as a way to record pictures of my favorite climbs. It had also helped me, on occasion, learn more about the mountains I was climbing and discover a whole community of people who were out there embarking on similar endeavors. Somehow it made my hours of isolation in the woods feel a lot less lonely. *Score one for social media.*

It was also helping me get comfortable writing for others. With each post, it became easier to share bits and pieces about my adventures, however funny or embarrassing they may be, and I found my writing growing in the process. How strange that something so ostensibly superficial as Instagram could help me develop what I want to say and how I want to say it. The more I posted, the more I wanted to write, and the freer I felt to express whatever was on my mind. But now, watching this scripted effort for likes, I wasn't so sure I wanted to be on Instagram anymore.

I looked over at Chloe who was staring at the women the way people look at roadside accidents, her mouth suspended in disbelief. She was as baffled as I was, trying to determine what strange lunacy had befallen them. When she finally spoke, Chloe said, "Hey Dad, you know what would be funny? We should Instagram a photo of those crazy girls on Instagram!" *My daughter is so cool. So very, very cool.* We got seventy-seven likes poking a little fun at the yoga ensemble.

But we were only poking fun. I respected the effort and the bonding, even if the way they chose to enjoy nature was quite different from how I like to experience it. A lot of hard-core outdoor enthusiasts revile "different" types of hikers, especially those flocking to popular destinations like Monadnock. They ridicule others' lack of preparedness for a big hike, and mock those who are clearly physically unfit for such an undertaking. They roll their eyes at an Instagram selfie session, which I admit, I have done many times, finding it hard to stomach all that self-adulation while they miss out on the world around them. But at least this selfie session got them out there. Anyone making the effort to drag their bones up a mountain indicates a desire to improve themselves, body and soul, and that's good enough for me.

What counts is the effort. I take my kids up mountains to impress upon them that from effort, comes reward. Standing at the summit of a mountain, taking in awe-inspiring views that reveal the vastness of the earth and the minuteness of our presence, is the easiest way I know how to teach them that. And it's ok to have a crowded mountain experience from time to time; it lets you know that there are many others out there, valuing effort as well.

The shared effort of achieving a mountain summit bonds people together, because it lets you know a little about the other person's resolve. Knowing someone else's ability to persevere over miles of rocks provides comfort that you can count on someone else besides yourself in this life. It lets them know the same. Climbing with Liz up Mount Rainier, trekking over crevasses and enduring six days of misery-induced climbing, gave me all the assurances in the world that I married the right woman. Not once did she complain. Not when we woke up in the darkness for the early morning summit attempt. Not later when we got back to camp, our hands going numb from the freezing cold as we boiled snow to make drinking water for everyone. Not the next day when she woke to discover she had gotten glacial sunburn, and her lips had blown up like two frankfurter sausages. No complaints. Not once. I'll never forget that. Nor the fact that our daughter exhibited the same type of character on her very first big climb. The images are now forever linked in my mind.

A few days after Monadnock, I tackled Mount Carrigain at breakneck speed with my buddy Jonathan. From our previous climbs together, I knew that he was the right guy to share in that kind of effort. We ran most of the ten-mile stretch to bag this 4000-footer, and when we got back to where we were staying that afternoon, Jonathan hit the sack before sunset. *I think I actually tired him out.* This was saying something. Jonathan ran fifty-mile races and treated his body like a temple. He once ran the Loon Mountain Race with me, *backwards,* while cheering me on, and did it faster than me, much to my chagrin. The fact that I wasn't as tired as him encouraged me that I was ready for the next big push.

After so many solo ascents, getting out there with my daughter and my friend gave me a much-needed second wind for the last phase of my journey. It was also terrific to finally get to take some pictures of other people. I was so ecstatic about my hike with Chloe, I used twenty-five hashtags on the picture I posted of her at the summit of Monadnock—only twenty more than my Instagram coach Alicia advised me to use. I know posting for likes isn't model parenting, and I was very careful not to have a clear image of her face on my public profile in case there are any creepy weirdos out there, but what can I say? Sometimes I'm weak. How could I not give my daughter the most hashtags I've ever used? She'd been getting such a kick out of seeing the number of likes I got on Instagram that I wanted her to get the most likes her insta-challenged dad could muster. She got one hundred and forty-eight! She was psyched. Well, well, well, whose instagame was going up?

#mountains #thegreatoutdoors #neverstopexploring #exploremore #natureaddict #takeahike #getoutside #getoutthere #igersnh #nature #hiking #optoutside #getoutstayout #letsgosomewhere #monadnock #visitnh #getoutsidenh #hikenh #whitemountains #scenesofnh #outsideisfree #hikethewhites #scenesofnewengland #newhampshire

Chapter 23

Saint Dale?

Some dirt roads make you feel welcome, like you are embarking on a wonderful escape to commune with nature and find some inner peace. Others make you feel like there's a distinct possibility you could get shot by a deranged hillbilly, hopped up on moonshine and chewing tobacco.

At the end of the dirt road leading to the Mount Cabot trailhead, I came across a grass field littered with "No Trespassing" signs—too many to think any sane person placed them there. Looking at the surrounding landscape, it was clear that not many came this way. Google Maps said I was in the right place, but there was no indication of a trailhead anywhere. All I could see was tall grass and private property. My Spidey senses began to tingle.

Unsure of how to proceed, I pulled over onto a small patch of dirt to get my bearings and search for another option to ascend. There was only one. My map of Mount Cabot showed trails stemming from the Berlin Fish Hatchery, which was on the opposite side of the mountain but over thirty-five miles away by car. *Man, what a disaster.* Not wanting to waste time mulling it over, I shifted my truck into drive and was about to take off for the hatchery when a friendly-looking couple pulled up in a little Jetta.

The gentleman riding shotgun rolled down his window and the driver, an English lady in her late fifties, reached across. "Are you looking to climb Mount Cabot?" she asked, her accent full of promise and hope. *What is it about English accents that makes everything seem so rosy?*

"Yes," I told her, "but it seems I'm blocked." I pointed up the hill towards the "No Trespassing" signs.

"Oh, it's no problem," she assured me. "The property owner here closed off the road to try and keep it private, but you can still go up it anyway. Just walk straight up the middle, between the two houses there. Just ignore the signs and you'll be fiiiine."

Her sing-songy voice was persuasive, and I could feel myself giving into the idea.

"Really?"

"Yes, we do it all the time, no problem," she said.

"All the time" sounded promising.

The man in the passenger seat, a small but sturdy-looking fellow who had remained silent until now, decided this was a good time to finally speak. "Yeah, but you'll be all alone up there, though." *American.* And the way he looked at me suggested that it should probably be okay, but maybe it won't. Then they smiled; she said, "cheers," and he said, "good luck," and they left me in a swirl of dust and unanswered questions.

Replaying their advice in my head, I decided I needed protection in case there was some animal—or something else—out there. English lady inspired optimism, but American guy stimulated realism, and perhaps a little bit of fear. I always keep a toolbox in my truck for work, and from it I extracted my not-so-big, not-so-scary, Leatherman. A Leatherman, if you don't know, is a fancy Swiss-army-like knife with pliers, which, should I have the misfortune of running into a bear or worse, cannot unfold quickly enough to do anything before the disemboweling begins. Still, it made me feel like I wasn't entirely naked as I went in search of the trail.

Past the houses flanking the no trespassing zone, I entered a meadow, brimming with ticks and waist-high grass. My hiking shorts came with attachable leg sleeves, and I considered putting them on here, but after counting seven more "No Trespassing" signs interspersed among the trees, I decided it was better to get Lyme disease than risk taking some buckshot to the keester. Not until I was fully ensconced in the woods, did I feel safe enough to put my pant legs on.

The climb up reminded me of the movie *Romancing the Stone*, when Jack Colton navigates the rainforests of Colombia: it was wet, there was thick green vegetation everywhere, and it was steaming hot. Using my hiking poles as machetes, I bushwhacked my way through the

New Hampshire jungle. It was evident that nobody had been up this way in years. Felled tree branches and bushes plagued the trail, blocking all discernable paths. Hacking my way through another bush I started muttering: "Oh yeah, we do this all the time, fucking nice old English lady, with her sweet voice, making it all sound so nice and easy."

Flies were my constant escort, and every ten minutes or so I had to stop and knock a couple ticks off my legs. Despite the mass hysteria about the dangers of ticks, they're not too big a deal as long as you vigilantly check for them. Scour your socks. Your underwear. The linings of your clothes. I've had hikes where I've found ten or more crawling in and out of my socks, but I've never got any Lyme. *That I know of, at least.* Ticks didn't worry me. What *was* beginning to worry me though was lovely sounding womenfolk from England pointing men directly into harm's way. *Is this how British men got talked into entering WWI? "Go ahead love, yeah, you'll be fiiiiine. We'll put the tea on when you get back. Cheers then."*

Pondering the English, I recalled reading in one of Bill Bryson's works how the English hiker doesn't think anywhere is off limits. That in their world view, there is no such thing as trespassing, and that it's perfectly acceptable to tread on anyone's territory, even if it belongs to some madman who buys his "No Trespassing" signs in bulk from BJ's. *This was a bad idea. I could be on some lunatic's land. There is a reason for all those signs. Shit! This is not good. Bloody hell!*

I struck on, scything away at the overgrowth for a couple of hours until I finally emerged on a real trail, thank the gods, the old ones and the new. I decided right then and there that I wouldn't be returning via crazy man's trail of terrors, no matter how long it took me to find my car again. Instead, I consulted my phone for an online trail map and made my way for the ominous sounding "Unknown Pond Trail." Taking this route added a considerable distance, but was presumably flatter, and I figured that the worst-case scenario would require a road hike back to my truck. It was a plan inspired by fear, inappropriately supported by an overzealous belief in my ability to conquer distances. And thus, my fateful journey began.

Before I could start on my new course, however, I still needed to make summit, a goal that felt increasingly less important as I passed a creepy old cabin, a few shades south of Cabot's highpoint. I was aware of this cabin before setting out for Cabot, and I know many people camp there, but if you told me that half of those campers are never heard from again, I'd believe you. Not wanting to find any permanent residents haunting the premises, I took a quick peek inside and hurried on to the viewless summit. After doing all that work for no reward, I decided Cabot might be worse than Mount Hale. *Screw it*. I sped on, making my way to the "Bulge" and the "Horn," subpeaks with views, and the supposed access to the Unknown Pond Trail.

But where the Unknown Pond Trail was, I still don't know. A twenty-minute search down and over the side of the mountain revealed nothing—it was an apparent dead end. After uttering a curse or two, I begrudgingly returned the way I came until I saw a freshly made sign that read "Unmaintained Trail." It pointed towards the hairy mess that began my day. *Thanks. Wish someone could have told me that before!* Staring into the unmaintained abyss of crazy man's jungle path, I concluded once again that I didn't want to return that way. The trail had been rough and slick, and there were sections where your feet slid down and got stuck in two feet of mud. Injuries were likely. And, of course, I didn't want to run into whoever might be lurking out there.

Thankfully, cell service was still working, and my phone revealed yet another alternate route. I was standing on the Kilkenny Ridge Trail, and it looked like I could descend it before cutting back to my car via the York Pond Trail. The route included the three peaks of Terrace Mountain, which wasn't ideal, but they looked small enough, given my frustration. The problem was the added mileage. It appeared that I was adding about 12 miles of hiking, but still pissed about not finding the Unknown Pond Trail, my adrenaline was up, and I was feeling indomitable. Without a clear idea of how much distance I was actually adding, I readied my pack to leave.

At that moment, a hiker with a chalky complexion, wearing a red Izod and a bad haircut, came ambling up the trail. He looked like an office worker, mild-mannered and compliant. It turned out he was doing the 4000-footers also and I was grateful he came along, because unlike me, he was smart. He had a real AMC map in his hand. *Why didn't I do that?* I told him I was thinking about going down a different path from the way I came up, because of my difficulties with the old Cabot Trail, and his eyes went wide with panic.

"You came from down there?" he said, pointing to the "Unmaintained Trail" sign. I nodded and waited for him to explain his bewilderment. *What is this all about?* "I can't believe you actually climbed up that. The guy who owns that land is in a big fight with the federal government about people crossing his trail, so he decided to kill a moose, decapitate it, and put the severed head on a spike to ward off hikers!"

"Holy crap!"

"Yeah, you don't wanna go back down that way. No way. Not unless you want to be shot at. I mean, first shot's a warning, second shot will get ya!"

Holy shit! Decapitated moose heads? Fight with the government? Little miss "we do it all the time" forgot to mention these pretty little details.

"Boy, am I glad I bumped into you," I said. We introduced ourselves and Chris unfolded his map to help me scout out a course of action. It appeared that my plan to run it out and over Terrace Mountain looked reasonable enough, but we spent a few minutes double-checking the map to be sure. Once we were both satisfied, I thanked him for the consult, and we parted ways. It wasn't going to be pretty, but in theory, I could circumvent Crazy Man McGee and get back to my truck around nightfall. Having verified my idea with someone who was better prepared, I was confident this new plan would work.

The extra miles up and over Terrace Mountain were of mild effort, and as I took a right onto what was supposed to be the start of the York Pond Trail, I was feeling pretty good. But only a few steps down the trail, I ran into a blockade of broken trees and more overgrowth. Wading around the first set of fallen trees, it was obvious that they were cut on purpose in a deliberate effort to cover up the trail. Bushwhacking was no use; the whole trail was sabotaged. Then it hit me: *this was probably the beginning of Crazy Man's land!* My adrenaline spiked.

The day was getting short and I found myself caught between two choices: risk the ten miles down the York Pond Trail to my truck, hoping to find a way through the death maze of trees and brush, or sprint two and a half miles to the completely opposite side of the mountain to the hatchery, and hopefully hitch a ride with someone. *Maybe I can catch up with Chris!* If I couldn't, I was screwed.

I took off like a bat out of hell. Even though it was July, the trail to the hatchery was brown and decaying, and I spurred myself on, hopeful there was life at the end of the tunnel. Despite my heavy pack, I ran the distance in less than twenty-five minutes, and when I found the hatchery parking lot, I spotted Chris getting into a red sedan. "Hey Chris!" I'd travelled eight miles since I left him, while Chris had hiked three, and he was astonished by my presence.

"How did you get here so fast?" he asked.

Chris's eyes went wide again as I explained what happened at York Pond. Positive that Crazy Man had blocked off the route, Chris offered me a ride before I got the chance to beg. Driving out towards civilization, I learned we had a lot in common, except for the fact that he was a better planner while I was willing to risk extra miles at the drop of a hat. We chatted about his work as an analyst, and although there was nothing too interesting covered in our conversation, I kept thinking that his car felt like kindness. Chris was able to drive me twelve-and-a-half miles to Berlin, where he dropped me off at an Irving gas station; he had to head north from there, whereas my journey continued south towards Gorham. If he was going my direction, he said he would have taken me the rest of the way.

At the station I asked the attendant if there was any bus heading to Gorham, and incredibly there was, but the last one for the day left over an hour ago. Getting desperate I asked, "You don't know if there are any cabs, or even an Uber around, do you?"

The attendant smiled and said, "Nah, we don't have nothing like that up here." I didn't know how to get an Uber even if there was.

A Dr Pepper and a Gatorade in hand to fuel up, I dropped my behunker down on the curb outside and called mission control. "Hey Shoog. Just calling to let you know I'm okay. Sort of having a weird turn of events here . . ." I looked at my phone while I talked, mapping out the remaining distance. I wasn't exactly sure, but it looked like I had about thirty-three miles to go to get back to the car. *Thirty-three miles?!*

With no bus, cabs, or Uber available, and knowing nobody within a hundred square miles, I had no choice but to resort to something I hadn't done in twenty-two years, back when I was walking the mean streets of Nantucket. When I was sixteen, my buddies and I hitchhiked the

Milestone Road to Siasconset, where we got picked up by a drunk who let us saddle up in the back of his pickup. Halfway down the road, we realized the guy was lit, as the truck was swerving all over the place, and I swore I'd never hitchhike again after that. If hitchhiking in the safest island hamlet in the world felt dangerous, what could I expect to run into in the nether regions of New Hampshire?

My thumb was out for half a mile before a rusty blue pickup slowed down and gave me the once-over. When it pulled past me into a Sherwin-Williams parking lot, I was relieved the driver didn't offer me a ride. The truck's battered bodywork, the sunlight obscuring the driver's face as it reflected off his window, the slow roll to check me out—all of it felt like the beginning of an episode of *Unsolved Mysteries*, one I didn't want to star in. A few minutes later, my thumb back in my pocket, the same blue pickup rattled up alongside me. Inside was a toothless, hollowed-out man who offered me a crooked smile and said, "Need a liff?"

I was torn. Including the road hiking, I had already hiked for some twenty miles, and still had at least a marathon to go. That wasn't appealing in the slightest. On the other hand, I didn't want to end up chopped into tiny pieces, thrown into a garbage bag, and dropped in a ditch somewhere. *Decisions, decisions.* I opted for the grizzly death. "Are you sure?" I asked.

"Which way you headed?"

"Past Gorham."

"I'm going to Conway, I'll take you to Gorham." At least that's what I think he said. It sounded more like,

"I'magonna Conwaay, I'll techya Grum." Not wanting to be rude by asking for a translation, I opened up the passenger door and hopped in, thanking him profusely and introducing myself. I figured if I showed him how grateful I was, and that I had a name, he'd reconsider murdering me.

"Hop in," he said, "I'm Dale."

Dale turned out to be a pretty good guy. Toothless and maybe a little drunk, but a good guy. I couldn't understand half of what he was saying but from what I could glean, he came up to Berlin from Conway to check out a store. The paint store, I presumed. That was pretty much all I got. Looking around the truck, I thought it would be a miracle if we made it another mile. I mean this thing was a real beater. Dale was in a talkative mood and while he rattled on about his adventures, I looked for weapons. I saw paint buckets, old tools, and a dashboard that looked like it would break in half with one good kick. But no weapons.

Dale kept looking at me and smiling a lot when he spoke, and I nodded and feigned laughter to keep things simpatico. When he popped a cigarette in his mouth, any chance of understanding him went completely out the window, along with the plumes of smoke. At the intersection of Route 16 and Route 2 in Gorham, I asked Dale if he could pull over at the gas station on the corner. Stepping out, I thanked him for the ride, happy to escape with my life—not because I was still nervous about being murdered, but because I couldn't believe the truck didn't blow up. At the Citgo station I grabbed a couple more

Gatorades and began the march down Route 2. *Only twenty-five miles to go.*

A mile and a half down the road, a portly man in a Buick leaned out his window and said, "I'd give you a ride, but I live right here." Then he pulled into the driveway right in front of me. *Well, isn't that the worst nice thing to say.* He waved to me again as he got out of his car, and I told him, "No worries." After walking another mile or so, I realized what a huge idiot I was. *I should have offered to pay that guy for a ride!* At the top of an overpass bridge, I came to a halt and contemplated my options.

It was hot and I was tired. The best estimate I could get from my draining smartphone was that I still had twenty-four miles to go. *How can that be?* With already more than twenty-two miles of hiking behind me, I was gassed. I looked west towards my car, then east from whence I came. West. Then east. West. Then east. I decided to go back east and beg the guy with the Buick to let me pay him. But before I could take a single step, a red pickup came barreling toward me, smoke billowing from its engine hood. When it came to a haphazard stop about thirty feet past me, I sprinted up the highway to catch the driver. "Thank you for stopping!"

The man was gritty, dirty, but handsome in a rugged way, with a taut frame carved out by years of hard labor and cigarettes. "Saw you walking there and wanted to give you a lift. Hope I can do it. Know anything about engines?" As he hopped out of the driver's seat, I noticed he was barefoot.

He popped the hood and we watched together as steam billowed out. "Overheating," he said. Then he asked me if I knew anything about radiators or engines or anything else it might be.

Not having the foggiest, I said, "I'm not really sure," and then bobbled my head back and forth like one of the IT consultants I used to work with. He crawled under the engine block and I decided to poke mine under too, hoping to God this guy could figure it out and give me a ride. *I really wish I knew more about cars.*

After fifteen minutes of poking around the outside of his truck like I knew what I was looking for, he decided it was okay to proceed at a low gear and a low speed. Closing the hood, he dropped a few more car terms on me and I nodded my head in understanding, but he could have told me he disabled the hyperdrive and I would have believed him. "Let's go," he said. Permission granted to hop aboard, I quickly introduced myself as part of my growing theory that if a highway killer got to know me personally, it would curb his bloodlust. "Nice to meet you Matt, I'm Chris." *No shit . . .*

It turned out Chris was a carpenter on his way back from filing divorce papers in Bangor, Maine. He said his "wife didn't show, of course," and now he had to get back to Vermont for a steel roofing job. He asked me if I minded if he smoked, and I said, "Not at all Chris, go right ahead." We made fast friends after that.

Chris stopped the truck ten minutes later to check out the smoke from the transmission fluid that was leaking out (his new theory). After inspecting it a bit, he concluded the truck would hold up until he got to a major town, and asked me what I was up to, hitchhiking all the way up here.

"Well Chris, I'm going through what you might call a little bit of a midlife crisis," I said, before explaining my goal of climbing the 4000-footers by forty. "Keeps me out of trouble," I joked. Then I told him about the disaster of a day that led me to him.

I expected him to make fun of me, but instead he sincerely said, "Well, good for you. Good for you for actually doing it. My hat's off to you, I think that's great. That's why you go on these adventures. Sometimes they work out for you, sometimes they don't, but you go on the adventure, that's good." Then he spoke of karma and how he was needing some of the good kind, which was why he picked me up. I'm not sure of the bad karma I deserved that got me into all this trouble in the first place, but good karma was certainly picking my ass up. I took note to pay it forward.

Riding with barefoot Chris and thinking of karma, a strange notion came over me. My three chauffeurs, total strangers that they were, had no desire but to help a fellow traveler without reward. They were all humble men, rambling about the world, largely unnoticed. If you walked by them on the street, you wouldn't give them a second thought. The first guy was a desk jockey that would be invisible at any cocktail party. The second was missing most of his teeth and looked like he rolled out of a storm gutter. The third was so hard up for work he had to travel two states away in a truck that could explode at any minute. But all three of these men seemed happy. Or at peace anyway. It gave me the strangest feeling that some saint, or perhaps a team of saints, was looking out for me. I eyed Chris a little more suspiciously.

Twenty miles down the highway we came to the turnoff that led to where my truck was parked. He asked me where to, but I told him it wasn't necessary; he had done enough, even though it was another six miles.

"Not at all, I'll take you all the way," he answered.

I was so grateful. But as we traveled the lonely dirt roads, I grew increasingly nervous. Hedging my bets, I thought it appropriate to inform Chris about where we were heading. I told him all about the decapitated moose head, the lunatic supposedly living there, and all of the "No Trespassing" signs. "So," I said, "hopefully my truck is still there and if it is, it's not shot to hell." *There, just in case Chris isn't a saint, he knows there is probably a crazy dude up here with a gun.*

Chris promptly replied, "Well, if it's been shot to hell, we'll shoot back." *Wait, what? Oh my God, he's got a gun. Of course he has a gun you idiot!* I scanned the interior of the truck again and rested my eyes on his glove compartment. *Maybe Chris only wants to take me up this dirt road so he can kill me where there won't be any witnesses.* I made a few more crazy moosehead-man comments, but it didn't matter. Chris was super nice and when we found my truck bullet-hole free, he waited to make sure it started before wishing me well and taking off. I think I offered him some gas money for his troubles, but he refused any compensation, saying karma was his reward, or something to that effect.

It felt so good to be back in my truck. Overall, I climbed seven distinct mountain peaks over ten ascents, hiked over twenty-two miles, and hitchhiked three times without waking up in a tub of ice with a kidney missing. Any day where you don't wake up in a tub of ice is a good day. After such a long trudge I had worked up quite an appetite, so on the way home I caught up with my dad at the 104 Diner in Meredith, to share a bite and a laugh about my misadventures.

Confessing my sneaking suspicion of saints among us, my dad, a Long Island boy who attended Catholic school growing up, told me about Saint Christopher, the patron saint of travelers. Saint Christopher, the story goes, stood over seven feet tall. Wanting to serve Christ, Christopher was instructed by a religious hermit to help people cross a treacherous river by carrying them on his shoulders. One day he carried a child, who proved to be particularly heavy. Christopher struggled mightily under the strain. Once he delivered the child safely to the other side of the river, Christopher commented on the surprising difficulty, declaring that it was the hardest crossing he had ever done. The child then revealed Himself as Christ and told Christopher that the reason He was so heavy was because He was carrying the weight of the world. My dad said, "So Matt, yep, I think you were escorted safely home by Saint Christopher himself." Only one question remained: Who the heck was Saint Dale?

Chapter 24

Pushing the Limits

I was pretty banged up. I had climbed eighteen miles over some of the most rugged terrain I could remember, and desperately needed a break. But I knew that if I didn't keep moving it would only get worse, so I barely paused to rest. The chairlift at the summit of Wildcat helped with my motivation. A full moon was out, and under its glow the chairlift looked like a spaceship harboring aliens. *Spooky.* Wondering if I might not be alone, my thoughts turned yet again to wolves, and I started singing loud enough to ward off any evil, from earth and beyond.

Despite my condition, things had gone, more or less, according to plan. Earlier that day, I set out with the goal of climbing the six 4000-footer summits of the Carter Range: Moriah, Middle Carter, South Carter, Carter Dome, Wildcat Mountain, and Wildcat "D." Parking at the

Pinkham Notch Visitor Center in Gorham, I purchased a one-way bus ticket and caught the first AMC bus out to the start of the Moriah trail. From there, the idea was to hike all the way back to my car via the "scenic route," traversing six 4000-footers and six additional peaks that, while not meeting the 4000-footer criteria, were still pretty damn big. The Visitor Center wasn't too far from the base of Wildcat, where I would ultimately descend, so I determined that I could get all six of the Carter Range 4000-footers done without having to expend extra energy backtracking over them to get to my car.

Starting early in the morning turned out to be a critical move. This was the hardest single day of climbing I've ever done, outside of Mt. Rainier. Up and over twelve peaks in *what I hoped* would be twelve hours, was no joke. Moriah confounded me from the get-go. Four times I thought I had reached the summit, and four times I was disappointed. The path was a rollercoaster of slanted granite, making for awkward steps that torqued my legs. By the time I made the summit of Moriah, my left knee was throbbing, and I was having trouble putting any weight on it. The "Tuckerman" breakfast sandwich from the Pinkham Notch Visitor Center wasn't sitting well with me either. My belly felt distended. Belch. Blech.

For the trip I brought six bottles of water and extra gear should I get lost or cold, making my pack noticeably heavier from my other climbs. Favoring my good knee to help with the weight, my steps were a little too lazy and I kept bumping into rocks and trees. It wasn't long before my legs were covered in scrapes. Blisters formed quickly as well, despite two layers of socks, and I broke open the first aid kit to tend to my wounds. By the time I reached my eighth peak of the day, which included four of the mountains on the 4000-footer list, I was bloody and famished. It felt like I needed more salt, but I had already run out of peanut butter goodies and trail mix. There was nothing to do but trudge on and try not to think about it.

In almost eleven hours of climbing, I didn't cross paths with too many people, but around 8pm, on my way up Wildcat, I ran into an overweight man in his sixties who was heading down the trail. He looked to be in pain, his knees buckling under the weight of his heavy frame as he descended the stony path. I asked him if he was doing okay, and he assured me he was. Unconvinced, I pressed him to see if he had a plan for the night, as if I, still heading up under a darkening sky, had any right to judge him. But he worried me.

"Yep," he said, "I'm going to head down a little further and then set up camp for the night." *Good.* He wasn't at all surprised that I was still going up. "Enjoy," he said.

"You too," I said, then watched in perplexed fascination as he plodded down the trail without complaint.

Night was coming fast, and I decided it was time to call Liz and let her know that I was okay, but things were taking longer than expected. There was only one problem. *No bars!* My phone had no cell service at all. On all of my previous climbs, I made sure to text or call Liz to let her know I was safe. She counted on hearing from me. With the sun going down and a long way to go, this was going to give her a heart attack. *Oh man, oh man.* Without any other option, I kept moving and prayed she didn't feel the need to alert Fish & Game.

By nine o'clock the sun had set, and I still hadn't bagged the two Wildcat peaks on the list. Even though I'd grown accustomed to descending after nightfall, it felt strange to be ascending in the dark. I had made some night ascents before, but that was with friends, never alone, and always as part of a guided trip. Nevertheless, as I caught the last bit of twilight in the valley below and watched the eerie moonlight prevail, I felt comfortable with my situation, and by 10:25pm I was standing at the alien transport on top of Wildcat D. I slowed my gait for a minute as I made my way down the grassy ski slopes, stunned by my surroundings, before the need for sustenance kicked back in, prompting me to charge for the vending machine I saw earlier that day at the Pinkham Notch Visitor Center.

Sometimes the mind can become so bent on a singular thought that it propels you to move faster and stronger than you normally move. The love for a child can make you stay up for two days with no sleep. The hope for a promotion at work can make you get twice as much work done as you typically do. The desire to become an expert guitarist can make you practice over and over again until your fingers bleed. And the desperate need for a Dr Pepper can make you truck down a 4000-foot mountain in roughly twenty-five minutes. I think it was twenty-five minutes at least. I could have been hallucinating from exhaustion and pain.

It took another twenty minutes or so to walk the road to the visitor center from the base of Wildcat. At the vending machine I didn't see any Dr Pepper, but I'd take whatever sugary substance it had to offer. *Fine, Vitamin Water.* I took out a couple of crumpled dollar bills and watched in horror as the machine ate them without giving me any credit. I ran back to my truck and grabbed some quarters to try again. The machine ate those too. Given that it was 11:30 at night and nobody was around, I yelled at the machine to "please give me a fucking soda!" That didn't work so I tried kicking it. I rocked it back and forth. I fonzied it. I yelled at it some more. The machine was unperturbed.

Phone service was still out, so I hopped in the truck and sped towards Jackson on a hunt for food, praying something was still open. Luckily there was. Thank God for the Circle K in Glen, New Hampshire. *Whoa, baby!* Inside, two women were laughing about all of the new disgusting food they were selling. They kept saying things like, "Who would eat these?" while holding a bag of potato chips loaded with delicious trans-fat. *Me, I would!* At that moment I would eat whatever disgusting food they had to offer. I loaded my arms with a Dr Pepper, a Coke, a ginger ale, a strawberry milk, a peach Snapple iced tea, a Snicker's ice cream bar, and to make myself feel a little better about my choices, a banana. I checked my phone again—still no service. *Weird. I guess I'll have to get to Conway.*

I inhaled my food, consuming everything but the ginger ale within minutes. By the time I reached North Conway, the carbohydrates were kicking in and brain function was slowly returning. I noticed several convenient stores were still open, as well as a McDonald's and a Taco Bell that was open twenty-four-seven, even though nobody was awake to eat. It felt like an odd business decision to be open twenty-four hours near a town with only a couple thousand people living in it, but it gave me great comfort to know I could grab a burrito at 3am if I had to. It was the only time I remember feeling truly grateful for modern consumerism.

With all of the business activity in North Conway, I realized that cell service was probably fine, and something must be wrong with my phone. Sure enough, when I rebooted it, my service came back on, and my phone lit up with voicemails from Liz, my dad, and a couple of friends, all wondering if I was still alive. I spoke to Liz and relayed my latest fiasco, telling her how sorry I was that I made her nervous. I really had her worried. My parents too. It was one o'clock in the morning by the time I let them know I was still among the living, and I felt terrible I had put them out so badly.

Heading down the Kancamagus Highway in the wee morning hours towards Lincoln, where I planned to stay the night, I reflected upon the day. I thought of how there were times when I cut my leg on another crag or slipped and fell on another piece of granite, and wondered why God cursed me so. *As if He had anything to do with it.* I recalled other times when I came across a seemingly unpassable stream, only to find that nature had provided a miraculous branch, positioned in just the right way to make a dry crossing possible. *Amazing.* I thought of how I brought the right amount of water, but probably needed a little more salt and sugar. *Noted*. But my biggest takeaway came from the moment I realized that I was going to climb in the dark without any cell service. Rather than rushing faster up the trail, I took a moment and stopped, slowing myself down to control my heartbeat and my breathing. Regaining my composure, I continued on confidently, and therefore safely. Like most situations in life, not panicking was the key.

Singing always helps too. Singing always makes me feel stronger. When I was scrambling up in the dark, trying to dig deep and make that next ascent, my body breaking down and my knees wobbling, it was hard not to sit down and rest. Hoisting myself up another boulder, these sad lyrics from Bear's Den popped into my head, where he is thinking of a mother he lost, and he sings, "You were a god in my eyes, you were a god." I started singing the chorus, "Don't cry, hold your head up high, she would want you to, she would want you to."

It made me think of my grandparents Frank and Eleanor, who recently passed away, and how they always represented to me the way people should behave. I never heard them complain or disparage anyone. I never heard them yell or disrespect anyone. They were funny, witty, and kind, and their quiet example made you want to stand taller for them. For your family. Thinking of them helped lift my body up the rocky path with more conviction and less complaint. Funny how the people who have impacted your life enter your consciousness in ways, and at times, you never expected. It makes it impossible to believe that their spirits ever die.

Okay, confession time. Fundamentally, I'm a Christian, but I believe in reincarnation too. I'm not sure how that would jibe with Heaven, but maybe Heaven is the final stop we can earn after a few good spiritual progressions on our reincarnation opportunities. From physics we know that a body in motion stays in motion, but what about the energy of a human spirit? How can that energy not transfer into something else? It can't dispel into nothingness, can it? That seems more remarkable to me than the alternative. Whether you believe in Heaven or reincarnation, or you are an atheist, or whatever you believe, the universal faith we should all have is that it is entirely possible that whatever brought us here could escort us back home again. Right? I mean why not? The probability of your existence is so minute, why deny yourself the idea that some force could convert your spirit into something else? Oxygen converts to carbon dioxide. Carbon dioxide converts back to oxygen. Is it different oxygen because the conversion of carbon dioxide makes it something different? Or is it the same oxygen, returning from a miraculous trip?

Chapter 25

The Presidential Traverse

It was time for the big one: a climb over the Presidentials of New Hampshire, all in one shot. The Presidential Traverse is the most heralded of the 4000-footer hikes, with five of the ten largest mountains in New Hampshire, including Washington, Adams, and Jefferson. Spanning twenty-three miles of hard scrabble, roots, mud, and rock, it's the ultimate New Hampshire climbing bucket list challenge. If lucky enough to get above the treeline on a clear July day, your reward is an unobstructed view of a stirring expanse of massive peaks, running in a crest from north to south.

With wobbly legs and a foggy head, I began—the result of allergy medicine and a lack of sleep. But I woke right quick when I came across a woman relieving herself in the woods, no more than a mile up the trail. Despite being half-asleep, I was still off to my usual fast-paced start, giving her no time to react to my sudden appearance. Squatting over a large flattop boulder, she let out a mousy squeak as I came around the bend. "Whoa!" I shouted, throwing my arms up in the air and jumping behind a tree. "I didn't see anything!" I assured her. *Nice Matt, I'm sure that's exactly what she wants to hear.*

After a minute of fumbling about to finish up, she giggled and gave me the all-clear to pass. Proceeding with caution, I kept my head down so our eyes wouldn't meet, hoping to save us both from any further embarrassment. She kept her back turned to do the same. Twenty yards later, I bumped into her friend running lookout for anyone coming down the trail. *She didn't think someone might be coming up? And why didn't her friend get off the trail to do her business? What was she doing right in the middle of—?* A tremendous roar interrupted my thoughts. Believing a bear was upon me, I shot my hands out and braced myself for an attack. A military jet thundered overhead. Fighter jets performing training exercises in the White Mountains were common, but this one echoed off the surrounding valley with such a low rumble, it sounded animalistic. Two more jets passed overhead during my ascent of Jackson, and twice more I looked for bears before realizing what they were.

The hike up Mount Jackson was relatively easy. I suppose like anything else, the more you do something, the easier it becomes. When I first climbed Moosilauke (finally), the act of climbing a single 4000-footer felt like a major accomplishment. But then you have a day where you climb six. Today I was going to climb eight and Jackson felt trivial. No more than a speed bump. Now a master of the walking office, I spent time on the ascent calling customers, scheduling maintenance repairs, and even signed a couple of leases. All from my phone! When I reached the summit, I was prouder of being free from desk restraints, than for bagging another 4000-footer.

On the other side of Jackson's summit, I came across the AMC's Mizpah Spring Hut, where sane people stop to break up their hike and enjoy a night's stay in the mountains, complete with prepared meals from the hut's staff (mostly college kids enjoying summer gigs). Even though I wasn't staying there, I went in to replenish my water supply, which the staff let me do at the kitchen sink. Having the huts along the traverse is a huge advantage because you don't have to carry the same amount of water you typically would on such a long hike. This made my back very happy.

Back outside, stocked up and feeling energized, I started up the path towards Mount Pierce, where I could hear the odious sounds of complaint emanating from the woods ahead. "Why, Dad? Why did you make me do this?" came a voice. "Why did you bring me here?" I could hear sobbing and the smacking of aluminum on wood. Rounding the corner, I found a father-son team, Italian and overweight, huffing and puffing their way as they hauled large overnight packs up the rocky path. We were only ten minutes away from the hut, where I presumed they stayed the night before, and the son was already losing his mind.

Without looking back at the boy, the father said, "Because this is good for you. Look at Tommy, he's already up the trail. You can do it." The son, who had to be at least eleven or twelve years of age replied, "No," and plopped himself down on a rock, his arms folded across his chest like he was a three-year-old refusing to eat. Dad, already overloaded with his own pack and another bag that probably housed the chubby little ingrate's video game console, turned around with an exasperated look. Trying his best to be supportive, he suggested taking his son's bag too.

I couldn't believe it. This poor guy looked to be a hundred and fifty pounds overweight and was now going to saddle himself up with whatever else the little wretch was schlepping? *Tell the kid to get his ass up.* I really felt for the guy. He probably had this great vision of the mountains giving him and his son a chance to bond. A chance for his son to build some character while laying off the twinkies. But the son wasn't having any of it.

It sometimes feels as though kids like this are all you hear about these days. Kids that are spoiled, adrift, and helpless. And so unhappy. How ironic that kids are so unhappy, diagnosed with more anxiety and depression than ever before, even though their parents worry about their kid's happiness twenty-four-seven. Could it be because they don't feel in control of their own lives? Throw a backpack on them, send them to the woods and treat them like adults, and my guess is they will eventually start talking and smiling, even if they complain the whole way. Most kids will, anyway. This kid looked like a particularly hard case, though. The dad had the right idea, only an impossible pupil. Twenty minutes after passing the father-son duo I found the aforementioned Tommy, who asked me if I'd seen his companions. I assured him that they were coming, but it didn't look good for his pal. He gave a nod and grimaced, signaling he knew full well what a pain in the ass his buddy can be. Tommy's going to be fine.

The eight 4000-footers of the Presidential Traverse are Jackson, Pierce, Eisenhower, Monroe, Washington, Jefferson, Adams, and Madison. Jackson, while sharing the name of a former president, is actually named for New Hampshire geologist Charles Jackson. But most people don't know this, so Jackson gets thrown into the mix as a "Presidential." The rest of the mountains are in fact named for former presidents, with Washington, Adams, and Jefferson claiming the 1-2-3 spots in height, in line with their presidential order.

Having climbed Washington and Jefferson before, I more or less knew what to expect from these, but I wasn't expecting the beauty of Pierce and Eisenhower. *How come nobody talks about these?* Pacing north along the ridge, some southbound hikers smugly told me I was going the wrong way because southbound was "way prettier." Watching them descend from where I came, I had to agree. The views were stunning, and it made me wonder why Mount Pierce didn't get more press. After all, the man himself was the only president to come from New Hampshire. Then again, he is also regarded by many historians as being one of the worst, if not the worst, president of all time. My vote is for Buchanan, but that's me.

Even though it was to be an eight-peak day in terms of the 4000-footers, fifteen separate peaks were actually on the menu when you factored in the subpeaks interspersed along the traverse, as well as two additional mountains in Franklin and Clay. By the time I got to the sixth peak of the day, Franklin, I was feeling the wear and tear. During the climb over the Carter-Moriah range, my left knee was giving me trouble; today it was my right. Perhaps the result of favoring it so much during the previous week's trek. To help with the pain I developed a little mantra: *My legs are light. My legs are light. My legs are light.*

Liz and the kids were planning on meeting me at the summit of Mt. Washington for lunch. Washington sits roughly at the halfway point of the traverse, so it made for a great meetup spot because Liz could drive to the summit up the Mount Washington Auto Road. After a morning of scouting and dropping into swimming holes around the town of Gorham, they drove up to the summit in our Honda Odyssey, the official car of every couple who has traded in their street cred for comfort. The kids found the mountain road terrifyingly steep and narrow, and were convinced that the minivan was going to roll right off the edge of the mountain.

As I approached the summit, Liz and the kids were already there, and they hiked down a hundred feet to greet me. It was the best. After having climbed so many steps alone, nothing could have made me happier. We sat and looked out at all of the mountains stretched before us, the kids in disbelief I had done all of the ones I pointed to. We took pictures and they commented on my tank top and my arm muscles. I was wearing an orange headband from a Tough Mudder competition and my mountain sunglasses from EMS, and the kids thought I looked pretty cool, which was very, very cool. Having your kids think you are cool for a nanosecond is worth the slog up any mountain.

If my family was not there to greet me, Washington's summit would have been a real disappointment. After enjoying a full year of majestic views, serene hours of isolation, and so many great interactions with wildlife and friendly hikers, Washington was an eyesore, mobbed by tourists sucking down extra-large cokes and standing in line to take pictures of themselves in front of the summit sign. *You should have to earn that right.* It felt a little like Disney.

After a half-hour lunch break, I wanted to get going. Even though there were only three major peaks left to do, they were the longest ones, and I knew it would take the rest of the day. When I summited Jefferson, I didn't waste much time enjoying the view; the summit is a heap of rocks that are not terribly comfortable to take a break on. I sat for a brief moment on a wobbly piece of schist and considered myself availed of having to give Jefferson any more of my time. I've always found Jefferson to be a little overrated anyway.

Years ago, Liz and were attempting a two-peak day of Adams and Jefferson, when we got socked in by fog and had to settle for Jefferson alone. Adams is one of my favorite presidents, if not my favorite, and I regretted missing my chance at going to the mountain named in his honor. I'll spare you the full historical recap, but for everyone who thinks Jefferson or Washington were the greatest, it can be argued that neither of them would have risen to such prominence without the undying support of Adams. It was Adams who promoted Washington to be the first president, and it was Adams who ensured that Jefferson wrote the Declaration of Independence. Nobody likes Adams because he was a crotchety little grump, but I'm telling you, he was a force. Him and his son were also the only two presidents of the first ten that didn't own slaves. Look it up y'all. Facts.

Crossing the ridgeline from Jefferson to Adams, I noted that Mount Adams was fairly similar to Mount Jefferson, and yet I was so much happier taking my time at the summit, simply because of my respect for its namesake. While I took in the views from Adams, three guys in their twenties were settled in among the rocks, snacking on protein bars and sandwiches. I plopped down next to them with my Payday and a Gatorade. "Which way you guys heading?" I asked.

Their leader replied that they had spent the night at one of the huts and were going to do a second night at the Madison hut, which was the direction I was going. "You come from Washington?" he asked.

"Yes, well, started the day at Jackson."

His eyes bulged. "You started at Jackson?"

"Yeah."

"Wait, today?"

"Yeah." His buddies looked up at me. All of them were a few inches taller than me, built, and young.

"Holy Christ dude, this is our second day, and we are gassed." I looked at all of them and they did look like a whooped bunch. Seeing how far I'd come with my fitness and my ability to bang out mountains relative to a bunch of guys in their twenties made me feel like a flipping rock star. I chatted them up for a few more minutes and then left them in the dust.

But in reality, I was pretty gassed as well. After making the final ascent up Madison I struggled mightily on the way down. The going was steep, and I remembered Jonathan telling me that when he had done the traverse, he started with Madison in order to get its sharp incline over with early. When I made my plan for the traverse, I decided that I could conserve energy by starting with Jackson and working my way up more gradually, tackling Madison on the descent. I came to regret that decision.

The familiar ache of bone grinding on bone settled in my knees again, and once more I found myself hiking in the dark. Knowing that Liz and the kids would be in the parking lot waiting for me, I started to run with my headlamp on, down the Valley Way Trail. No longer afraid of the dark and what creatures might be lurking about, I didn't sing, and I wasn't running out of fear. Running was purely a time thing.

With about a mile left to go I heard a small voice yell, "Hello?"

"Chloe?" I yelled back.

"Dad!!" *The kids!*

Never one for patience, Liz decided to take the kids up the trail and see if they could intercept me. They had no headlamps, flashlights, or food, but there they were, a mile up the trail, wandering around in the dark. The kids were so excited to find me; it was the cutest. But it was also the worst because they kept walking in front of me like a pack of Labrador Retrievers looking to get fed, tripping me up as I struggled to alter the progression of my battered legs. Over that last mile my legs completely stiffened up as I tried to get the kids to move a little more quickly. It would have been much faster, and less painful, if I could have jogged that last mile and be done with it, but I didn't mind. Having Liz and the kids with me made me feel so whole, I didn't care if my kneecaps exploded and my feet fell off. What more does a man need than a family to love?

Back at the car, Liz had a Dr Pepper waiting for me and I gulped it down as I rested my dirty, aching feet on the dashboard. The kids talked all at once, unable to contain their enthusiasm for the experience of meeting me up the trail in the dark. They recounted the events of the day and detailed all of the swimming holes they explored while waiting for me to finish the trek. Listening to them, breathing in every word, I felt my body totally relax, knowing most of the hard effort was done. There were only six mountains left to climb on the list, and I had seven months to go before I would turn forty. I didn't even really care if I completed the list now; I was deeply satisfied.

Chapter 26

Thoughts Over Ice Cream and Beer

Before I met Liz, the love of my life was ice cream, and ohhh did we have a good time. Sweet, sweet ice cream, nobody can hate you. And beer. Beer was pretty good too. After I completed the Presidential Traverse, I no longer had the burning need to knock off mountains and felt I deserved a little ice cream. Well, a lot of ice cream.

Growing up I would often polish off a quart of ice cream for dinner. It was a habit I fell into when I'd come home late from school, and nobody was around. Some nights I'd have a microwave pizza for dinner, some nights I'd make pasta, and some nights I'd throw a quart of ice cream in a salad bowl and down the whole thing while watching an episode of *The Simpsons*. It was fantastic.

When Liz and I climbed Mount Rainier in 2005 with my sister-in-law and her husband, they all confessed that they didn't quite believe I was going to make it. Back then I was twenty-eight and my diet hadn't evolved much since I was a teenager, except that I had added beer to the mix for further nutritional support. Despite my poor eating habits, I wasn't too out of shape, but perhaps a little portly, with a bit of a fat tire that I subconsciously sucked in all the time.

Eventually, through marriage, my diet steadily improved, and I cut back on ice cream and beer even more during my quest for the forty-eight. But now I let it all go to hell. Black Raspberry, Caramel Delight, Dulce de Leche, I mean come on! So good. Since college I only ever drank a few beers on the weekend, so that didn't change much, but my ice cream intake tripled. Within a month I gained ten pounds, and I was so very, very happy.

The whole month of August I did nothing but relax. I took my kids to soccer camp during the week and out sailing on the weekend. We taught the kids how to operate a motorboat, explored the beaches of Maine, and hit up Lake Winnipesaukee with the cousins. I read a bunch of books about adventures in the White Mountains and the hardships people faced while climbing. But mostly I ate ice cream. I almost got through the entire month without thinking about my unfinished business in the mountains, but by August 30th, I was no longer content to "just be." *Why couldn't I relax one more day?*

With each passing year I have a harder time "just being." Perhaps it's because nowadays I spend most of my time on the sidelines, watching our kids play soccer while chitchatting with other adults about the Patriots and the next barbeque we're going to have. I can do this for one game, but a whole season of it? It was boring discussing the Patriots even when they were good. I want adventure and I'm struggling to fake it through the mundane. I've got to keep doing new things. I can always find something next to do. Only in doing am I totally content with my being.

If I'm not working on something at my desk, then I've got to be working on my house, or on one of the building projects I have. If I've done all of my work-work, then I need to climb a mountain. If I don't have a mountain in mind, then some other adventure ensues. As long as I'm building, I'm happy. Each day is an opportunity to build. Some days you get to build upon your career. Some days you get to build upon your relationship with your kids, your wife or loved ones. Some days you get to build upon a personal goal you set for yourself, like climbing a bunch of rocks in New Hampshire. And even though I don't think we should idle too long and get stuck in self-reflection, I do think it's important to meditate and take time to exercise in some way every day, making sure to reflect upon where you're at so that you can build upon your developing character.

I wasn't always like this. Hanging out and "just being" is no problem when you are a teenager, or even in your twenties, because you are not yet attuned to the diminishing timer set on your life. In your youth you have time to waste on indulging your ego and getting lost in self-reflection without having done anything to reflect upon. But it's a mistake, at any age, to convince ourselves that simply relaxing, and "just being," is the way to get in touch with our real selves. Only by doing and engaging with the world around us do we discover who we really are. What we love. What we care about. What we do or don't like. What we want.

I fear for this next generation of children, their eyes glued to iPads and smartphones while helicopter parents hover above them. Where is the time for them to be free to think? To experiment and build? To be alone with their thoughts? To have a little hardship and figure things out on their own? Some hardship is good. Seems likely to me that this modern society is robbing our children of their opportunities to develop resilience.

I often worry whether I am doing a sufficient job to help foster my own kids' ability to navigate this strange world we're living in, because their childhoods are notably different than my own. For starters, I work from home, so my kids see me a lot. Like, all the time. When they leave for school, I'm there to walk them to the bus stop or say goodbye. When they get home, they can run up to my office and see if I want to play in the backyard with them. And of course I do. I love that I can be this accessible to them. But I often fear that by being ever-present, I'm giving them a crutch that's going to disable them in the future.

When I was a kid, my dad was already long gone by the time I woke up, and I frequently never saw my mom all day. I'd make my breakfast, get picked up by my carpool, and off I'd go. As I got older, I could go days without having much interaction with either of my parents at all.

This was partly because I was a teenage boy with all of the spacey innerworkings that come with that, but some of it was because my parents were simply out and about, doing their own thing. My dad worked all the time and my mom was very social, heavily involved in the community, whereabouts unknown.

In the days before cell service and Life360, finding mom was damn near impossible, and relying on her for a ride was an exercise in humility. She was a logistical nightmare of epic proportions, her proclivity for missing pickup times the stuff of legend, openly discussed at dinner tables all over town. I was usually the last one waiting in the parking lot for pickup. Always the last kid getting dropped off. Sometimes it was a little unclear if someone was coming to get me at all, so I'd bum a ride from someone else's mom. My dad gets a big kick out of the image of me wandering around during my childhood, wondering how I was going to get home, and says, "See, your mother must have known what she was doing, because you turned out okay." Waiting around certainly helped me learn to enjoy my own company, but I would have much preferred a predictable ride.

I am fully aware that my life as a parent is a reaction to my life as a child. I coached my sons' youth baseball games because I wished my dad could have made it to more of my games. I'm always on time for everything, even early, because I hated always waiting to get picked up. But while my parenting style may be a reaction to things I didn't like as a child, it's also a reaction to what I think worked. At times I'll push the kids towards doing things on their own so that they get over their fears and learn how to cope. Most of these situations revolve around having to speak to an adult or interacting with a bunch of new kids for the first time. New experiences can be awkward and painful, but if introduced with the proper support, can be immensely helpful building blocks of resiliency. With practice, the easier it gets to roll with any kind of punch.

My parents were also great teachers of history and showed me a broader world. They have keen senses of humor and are great storytellers. Life with them was never boring. They took me on great trips and discussed things with me like I was their intellectual equal. Their insights taught me more about life than anything I learned in school, and I'm inspired by their example to pay it forward to my kids. I'll be lucky if I can invigorate my children's learning half as much as my parents did mine.

Barring some crude exceptions, each generation of parents tries to improve upon what was given to them. You take what you think your parents did right, throw out the parts you could have done without, and come up with your own recipe for the parental stew. Your kids will do the same thing with the lessons you're imparting and will devise their own set of best practices for raising their kids. And there's no way of knowing if the corrections you made are simply newfound mistakes. All you can do is stay in shape and, hopefully, someday meet your grandchildren to make amends for the errors in judgment you're making right now. *Dangit. I guess I should put down the ice cream and get climbing again.*

Chapter 27

Identifying the Enemy

Little mountains are mountains too, and after a month of sloth, I decided to reinitiate my climbing legs by tackling Rowe and Gunstock, two mountains situated in the Belknap Range. With summit heights under twenty-three hundred feet, you would think I'd have no problem after all the 4000-footers I climbed, but I struggled up their slopes. It was amazing to see how out of shape I could get after one month of eating ice cream.

To be fair, Rowe started off steeper than expected. On the way up, I actually walked past a guy trying to ride up the trail on a mountain bike. No matter how fast he pedaled, he couldn't keep pace with my lethargic steps and eventually fell from sight. *Well, that's a first.*

It was a morning of firsts, because shortly thereafter I came upon a cottontail rabbit, darting back and forth on the trail ahead of me. I'd never seen a cottontail in New Hampshire before, and I quickened my pace to keep track of it until I came across a raucous gathering of birds. Enveloping a thirty-square-foot radius of the riverbed running alongside the trail, they were raven black and cooing mightily as they vied for space on the river rocks. I'd never seen birds like these. I tried creeping up to them to get a better look, but the thick brush obscured their bodies, and I never figured out what they were. They sounded like mourning doves. Whatever they were, they kind of gave me the willies, so I moved on.

The whole hike felt weird. In addition to being caught off guard by the amount of effort needed to ascend, I was also surprised by how many people were out and about on the trails. I'd forgotten that the 4000-footers belong to a select class of outdoor enthusiasts and that smaller mountains like these are far more accessible to the average hiker. *Especially when the trailhead is located at an elementary school and school is in session!* Having grown accustomed to empty trailhead parking lots, my plan was to drive to the trailhead in normal street clothes and then change into my hiking gear upon arrival. So, you can imagine my horror when I learned that the trailhead was next to a playground teeming with kids and watchful mothers. Changing in the driver's seat, I slunk down as low as I could in order to avoid detection—and an appearance on the evening news.

As I worked my way up Rowe, the sounds of children and their mothers echoing in the distance, I found myself missing the isolation of the 4000-footers. Rowe and Gunstock reminded me of the spiritual beauty, and solitude, that comes with more challenging experiences, and I spent the majority of the hike pondering which 4000-footer to tackle next. When I got back to the truck I pondered some more, and kept on pondering, right up to the moment when my truck blew out a tire along the highway.

A loud "pop" welled up from underneath my feet and the Honda Ridgeline veered violently into the left lane, spinning the steering wheel with uncontrollable force out of my hand. Fortunately, there wasn't another car in the lane next to me, or I imagine it would have been a terrible accident. Before the truck flew off the highway, I was able to quickly yank the steering wheel back to the right and maneuver onto the grass, a few feet past the breakdown lane. *Hey, great!* No really, I thought it was great. Rowe and Gunstock had not filled my adventure quota and changing a flat tire was going to be my chance to capture the day. But I was rapidly disappointed. For forty-five minutes I tried to pry the lug nuts off the tires, and for forty-five minutes I failed. They didn't budge. All sorts of doubts about my manhood came over me. *I struggled up little Rowe, and now I can't even change a tire? Am I really getting that weak? Am I really getting that old?*

My pride vanquished, I tucked my tail between my legs and called AAA. An hour later, a small round man in a beat-up Camry arrived on the scene. He told me it would be no problem, and I watched as he struggled with my tire as badly as I had. Feeling the honor of my masculinity somewhat restored, I said, "hard, isn't it?" He conceded there was nothing I could have done to get the nuts off because the auto repair shop had "machined them on too tightly." A traditional tire iron was useless, so he pulled out a massive self-levering crowbar, which wouldn't have done the job either if he hadn't jumped on it several times, employing the full use of his girth and experience.

A week later, still unconvinced that I wasn't losing my edge, I decided it was time to get back out there. Given my desire for less people on Rowe, a lengthy assault of Mount Isolation seemed like an aptly named target. But when I woke up at 4am, my first thoughts were, *Man, I've done 42 of these, waking up this early in the morning? And most of them in the winter? How the hell did I do this?* I was really impressed with the guy I was a month ago.

It can be slow to find your old form when you start something back up, especially if it's on the Glen Boulder Trail. The first couple of miles ran steep and I plodded along at a turtle's pace. Still, the trail was lovely, and I didn't mind the slowness of my body. Upon reaching Glen Boulder, I stopped to admire the fog hanging in the valley, obscuring civilization and the highway below. A view free of man's presence had me feeling grateful and I found myself saying out loud, "Thank you." To whom, I'm not sure. To Mother Nature? To God? To people for not screwing this up too? To maybe all of them.

Sitting down to enjoy the view, I noticed something else. Somewhere along the way I had split the crotch of my pants wide open, and a large swath of underwear was showing. I felt grateful again, this time because the path to Isolation, was indeed, one of isolation. Had anyone been coming up behind me, they would have gotten quite a show. I was bummed about the hiking pants though; they were the ones that I used on Kilimanjaro. Oh well, nothing lasts forever, I guess.

Despite my crotchless pants, for some reason, perhaps hubris, I decided to add the 5492-foot peak of the Boot Spur to the climb. The Boot Spur is a subpeak of Mount Washington and was a totally unnecessary detour of a few extra miles over uncomfortably dispersed rock. I rolled my ankles more than once. By the time I reached the summit of Isolation, my body was broken and drained. Stumbling along, the only reprieve for my feet was the mulchy softness of the Davis Path, where time turned the decay of fallen trees into a fine padding of woodchips. With hardly a glance, I used my ViewRanger app to confirm when I was standing on Isolation's summit, and then descended the worst trail ever devised in the history of New Hampshire trail making: The Rocky Branch Trail.

The Rocky Branch Trail sucks. It's rocky, muddy, slippery, and covered with falling branches. It's named for the Rocky Branch River, but apparently Tropical Storm Irene caused significant damage to it in 2011, and the trail was closed until 2015. By the time I hit it in 2016, there were still hundreds of downed branches to contend with. Of course, I didn't know all this at the time and simply thought the trail was for shit.

Fifteen miles deep into the hike I was pining for a Dr Pepper, but the trail serpentined back and forth, delaying my progress towards sugary goodness. Compounding my discomfort were the swarms of blackflies and mosquitos hovering about my head as I repeatedly tripped over roots and "baby head" rocks hidden beneath the mud. Countless branches and fallen trees maligned the trail, nicking me left and right, while scores of ticks latched themselves onto my socks. All the while, the sound of cars taunted me, an echo effect from the valley below making the highway sound closer than it was. I kept rounding a bend, assuming I was finally at the parking lot, only to find another round of dense forest and mud. The last hour of hiking went on for an eternity. When I finally reached the road, bloody and tattered, I promised myself to never hike that trail again.

My route for Isolation was a loop, and when I reached the end of The Rocky Branch, I still had a three-and-a-half-mile road hike back to my truck, which was parked back at the trailhead for the Glen Boulder Trail. Luckily, after a couple miles of hoofing it, a gentleman in a Volvo SUV spotted me and offered me a ride. Now fully and inappropriately accustomed to the ways of hitchhiking, I gladly accepted. Turned out he was another karma hunter, having received a much-needed ride the week before from a fellow hiker. Even though he wasn't driving the kind of broken-down pickup truck I had come to trust, the Volvo guy didn't murder me, and ten minutes later I was on my way home.

On the drive home, something felt off, but I couldn't put my finger on it. Normally, after a big hike, I felt some sense of completion, or even a little closure, as I moved one step closer towards my goal. But this drive felt different. Later that night, while logging my climb on Peakbagger.com, I perused some of the pictures that other people had posted of their Mount Isolation summits. None of them looked like the summit I stood on. Every picture had clear panoramic views, whereas I was encircled by trees at the location ViewRanger told me was the top. *That's weird.*

Crawling into bed at one-thirty, I spent the next couple of hours tossing and turning, combing my mind for answers, but it was no use—I needed the internet. A review of trail maps on my phone led to the discovery of a tiny spur trail that takes you another twenty vertical feet to the actual summit. In my exhausted stupor on the trail, hardly able to raise my head, I'd completely missed it. A horrific feeling crept up my throat as I realized that I had climbed fifteen miles for nothing. *Nothing!* I'd hiked the world's shittiest trail, climbed the Boot Spur for no reason other than greed, and had completely failed to summit the mountain I had come for. *I never stood at the summit at all?* A flurry of swears escaped me as I sat straight up in bed, startling Liz awake.

Public support for my mission turned a little icy after that. Later that week, giving me a skeptical eye over breakfast, Liz told me I was "obsessed with age" and that I was too down on people. Not sure how those two failings were related, but I guess she figured it was best to get everything that was wrong with me out at once. In my head, I conceded that accepting my age might be a problem. But too hard on people? *I love people!* I might comment to her about other's life choices once in awhile, but isn't that one of the perks of having a spouse? After my Isolation failure, Liz started getting pretty annoyed with my commentary, and I made a mental note to not disturb her REM going forward. *Probably should keep my opinions to myself for a few weeks, too.*

But her jabs about accepting my age couldn't be chalked up to sleep deprivation or general husband annoyance. I knew I had a problem. This mortality deal was weighing on me. In my twenties I felt like I was invincible, and I wanted to live it up as much as possible before I got old and turned (gasp) thirty. In my thirties, the meaning of life hit me smack between the eyes when Liz gave birth to our children. I was all too glad to disappear into social obscurity, raise my kids, and limit my risks of an early demise, making sure my kids are big enough to swim in this world before I go. I gave up dreams of sky diving and owning a motorcycle. I focused on my career and making sure there would be enough money for them to survive if I kicked the bucket. For an entire decade I thought about nothing but the welfare of my wife and kids, and my health and stress certainly suffered for it. There was so much happy worry.

With forty now round the bend, things were getting a little weird. I couldn't stop thinking about how it was possible that anything could kill me at any time, and that life is so short I better get living again before my chance is up. Forty meant death was resting on my shoulder, winking at me, reminding me I still had things to do. Reminding me that I would not live forever. Forty felt an awful lot like Psycho Guide shouting, "WE COULD DIE AT ANY MINUTE!" I was afraid, but of what, exactly?

Fragile are our lives. The week I failed Isolation my Great-Aunt "Popcorn" Mary, whose namesake came from the popcorn she made for me when I was a child, passed away. That same week, an electrician friend in his early sixties, who was six-foot-two and strong as an ox, died of a heart attack. Like the alpine flora along the ridges of the Presidential Traverse, surviving against bitter winds and arctic temperatures but easily killed under the trample of a hiker, our lives hang in a delicate balance.

The grim reality is that you can die or get hurt doing anything. I could have died in a car accident getting to the trailhead. Or falling down the stairs on the way to the kitchen. If you worried about all of the things that could kill you, you'd never leave the house. To really live you have to accept the fact that you are going to die. Once you accept the inevitable, you will not waste time fearing it. If you go around fretting about your imminent demise, you limit your ability to lead an exceptional life. Fear is an inhibitor. Fear of death, illness, or getting hurt, all constrain your ability to flourish. But even though I thought I was successfully managing those fears, Liz was right. My age was bothering me. Not for a fear of death, but of dying before I've done something worthy of the gift I've been given.

For longer than history can record, men have yearned to do something with that gift. To make a name for themselves. To do something special. To conquer lands and obtain power. To find deeper meaning, connection, and immortality in the face of inevitable death. Turning forty spurs those desires further as one becomes increasingly aware of his pending irrelevancy. A part of me is writing now, not for the money, but for the declaration.

Writing fills an intrinsic need to raise a flag and shout one time before I die, "I was here dammit, and I've got something to say about how we can clean shit up around here!" And if someday I'm getting interviewed by Meredith Viera about my harrowing two-hour descent of a mountain while being chased by a menacing black lab that I'm allergic to, feel free to call me out if I say that I never imagined my book would mean anything to anyone. Every author thinks their words are worth reading or they would never write anything in the first place. Then again, if nobody ever reads this book, I won't be ashamed. I'm not afraid to fail. Or die. I'm afraid to have not even tried.

Going through life, regardless of whatever challenge you are facing, you are always facing an invisible enemy. Whether it's writing a book or working your way through school or dealing with an insufferable boss—you name it—there is only one enemy you really have to overcome: the lesser you. The one who says, "Let's just be" or "It's too hard" or "You're not good enough" or "It's not worth it." The one who says, "You basically climbed Isolation, who cares if you were twenty feet shy of the summit. Nobody will know." Even though Liz, my parents, and everyone else I talked to about my Isolation failure said that as far as they were concerned, I climbed it, there was no doubt about what I was going to do. I knew the night I woke Liz up in bed. I would have to go back and climb Mount Isolation again, because twenty feet shy of the summit, was twenty feet shy of the truth. When it came down to it, it wasn't forty that I couldn't accept; it was the lesser me it potentially represented.

Chapter 28

Where the Path Leads

The night before I headed out to tackle the Owl's Head, Liz made me promise that I wouldn't get lost in the woods this time. She also made me promise that I wouldn't hitchhike or alter my plan again, requiring miles of road hiking along the highway. I promised to meet all of her demands, knowing full well I couldn't deviate: the hike to Owl's head is a one-way-in, one-way-out trek of 18.2 miles on public land, completely free of decapitated moose heads and "No trespassing" signs. There would be no boogeyman to run from this time.

At the crack of dawn, I was wogging down the Lincoln Woods Trail, hoping to quickly shave off the first three miles of the journey before any other hikers surfaced. Lincoln Woods is a very popular trail for hikers and sightseers, and chances were good that plenty of them would be out soon. It was October in New Hampshire, after all. Prime leaf-peeping season. I didn't need the throngs watching me being weird, lumbering down the trail with my half walk, half run approach.

Once I was miles deep into the woods, having successfully escaped any sign of humanity, I slowed my pace, then stopped to listen, and look. All around, chipmunks darted in and out of the leaves, rustling music up from the ground. A young mink made an appearance, exploding out of a pile of leaves, before scurrying into another pile thirty feet down the trail. *A mink!* I would have completely missed him if I was still wogging. Suddenly I was overcome with the realization that the last few climbs were so laborious, I hadn't paused enough lately to stop and enjoy the earth around me. *How reckless.*

Off to my right, the powerful Pemigewasset thundered past. Rolling over and around glacial erratics, it drowned out the surrounding landscape, its waters drawing all of my attention. Where the river creeps close to the trail, you need to double your concentration if you're to catch sight of a squirrel or hear the chirping of birds, but eventually I gave up the search and focused on the river. The Pemi's power drowns out the efforts of every living thing to be seen or heard, and I lingered for awhile as nature's noise machine flushed my thoughts.

Eventually, I returned to the task at hand: churning out miles without pain or exhaustion. These long climbs can put hikers through some pretty grueling physical and mental anguish. To climb, and really do anything well, I believe you have to be able to sometimes shut off the part of your brain that focuses too much on what you are doing. With a quiet mind, you can rely on your instincts and reflexes to do the focusing for you, and not succumb to exhaustion and pain. I think that's how the greatest athletes are able to endure a long boxing match or the hellish strain of a cross-country ski race.

But I was maybe getting a little too good at tuning out my mind, because five miles into the adventure, I got lost crossing the Lincoln Brook. The trail graded down to the water and appeared to cross it, but once I was on the other side, I ran smack into a wall of bushes and ledge. There was nowhere to go. It was Taylor Swift's fault. She had been singing "Can't stop, won't stop moving," in my head, over and over again for the last ten minutes, and completely distracted me. What can I tell you? My daughter has taken over the radio at home.

Rather than pressing forward, assuming the trail would reveal itself in time, I stopped and looked up and down the banks of the brook. A careful search revealed that the trail picked up again, twenty yards upstream. Surveying the area for a few more minutes, I couldn't find the gap in the trail or how I had gone astray. A whole section of the trail simply wasn't there. Nevertheless, I was back on track. A few minutes of investigation saved hours of mistaken hiking; a lesson imprinted on my mind forevermore.

The Lincoln Brook Trail felt like a treasure hunt. Its small winding path halts and breaks at different angles, and it's fun to navigate despite the dearth of views. At the end of it you link up to the Owl's Head Slide Trail, which requires a good mile of scree scrambling, your steps sending loose rock tumbling down the mountain as you make your way to the top. The tree-cloaked summit also offers little in the way of views, but halfway up the slide was one of the most beautiful vistas I've ever seen, especially then, when the poplars adopt the canary yellow of early fall. I took my time here to contemplate.

Back home things were good. Liz had forgiven me for waking her up in the middle of the night, and the kids were healthy and happy. But many people I love and know were hurting lately. Some wanted help, some didn't. Some were sick. Some were depressed. Some were making mistakes for their future. For thirty minutes I weighed what could be done for them. Should I call them? Visit them? Send them a message? Bring them somewhere? Take them out? Leave them alone? Can I help?

This was happening more and more. Mountains were not only becoming my refuge for how to deal with problems in my own life, but also a sanctuary where I could better recognize the needs of others over myself. Every mile hiked drew me closer to the realization that no matter what's in store for us in the afterlife, or wherever our energy or mitochondria or essence goes when we die, the key principle that should guide our lives is that we are here, and we are here to help. I reminded myself to make more of an effort to connect with people when I got back down the mountain.

On most of my climbs I carried this little black Swiss Army knife, and returning down the Loon Brook Trail, I decided I needed it for the first time. Not to defend myself from a coywolf or a bear, but to cut the underwear off my body. It was saturated in sweat and the chafe started killing me around the fourteenth mile. Too tired to go through the effort of taking off my muddy boots and strip, I loosened my shorts, reached in, and shredded my underwear to bits. I figured it was the quickest way to relieve my pain and make sure I didn't get caught in the nude by a fellow hiker.

For the final three miles back to the car, there were more hikers on the Lincoln Woods Trail than I could count. There were old people, young people, people with pets, overweight people, people in clothes too fancy for hiking—more hikers on one trail than I had seen at any one time outside the summit of Mt. Washington. There weren't too many friendly hellos either. I wondered if it was because these weren't real hikers, but tourists out for a "leaf peeping" tour. At a small footbridge was a line of foreigners snapping photographs, speaking in German, English, and French accents. Perhaps a little Turkish as well? I tried to say hello but most of them ignored me. The only friendly greeting came from an Asian guy hiking by himself. After a glimmer of recognition that I was up to something different than the jean-wearers taking pictures, he smiled and waved.

You don't see too many foreigners in the higher elevations of New Hampshire, except for the French Canadians, who turned up on half my climbs. The ones I bumped into were always thin, fairly good looking, and dressed like a blizzard was about to strike. While I was overheating in a T-shirt, they were bundled in layers of shells and high-quality puffy jackets, ready for the apocalypse. But they always greeted me warmly. Truly, with few exceptions, everyone I bumped into in the highlands was always friendly. Kindness must grow in accordance with the recognition of increased effort.

After a year's worth of friendly encounters on the trails, it felt strange to walk among so many people not returning my hellos. Somehow as the volume of people on the trail increases, our courtesy and reception of each other evaporates until we're not much better than the hoards bustling down a city sidewalk. Could it be that the more we live on top of each other, the more disconnected we become from each other? That the reaction to too many eyes is to look away and avoid eye contact? That when individual space is limited, we turn inwards to protect ourselves from others taking more of it? I decided to keep saying hello and offering a smile, regardless of reciprocation.

Despite the poor reception at the trail's end, when I was back in my car, driving home, I started getting psyched. Even a little slaphappy. A little voice in my head started singing "I climbed the Owl's Head, oh yes, yes, yes, I did." Usually, the endorphins kick in for me near the mountain's summit, but today it happened when I finally had the chance to rest and reflect on the day. *What a day!* On Owl's Head I became enamored with hiking for the sake of hiking again. How wonderful it was to be out and alive, not worried about completing a list, simply enjoying the day. The list was losing relevance.

Liz had been getting excited I was coming to the end of my journey, not because she wanted me to be done with it (well, maybe a little because of that), but she couldn't believe I had climbed so many mountains in such a short time. She wanted to get a taste, so the following week we went up to Artist's Bluff with the kids, which is a small peak in Franconia Notch. After that we checked out Frankenstein Cliff by ourselves, wandering around the trestle bridge used by the Conway Scenic Railroad.

Catching the hiking bug, the next day Liz suggested that we climb Potash Knob, which is a peak off "the Kanc" that I had been eyeballing my whole life. I'd been putting it off because there isn't any trail to the summit and much of the ascent is a straight bushwhack through the White Mountain National Forest. This wasn't too big a deal, though, until we were a few hundred vertical feet from the summit. There the trees grew so tightly together we had to walk sideways to navigate them, and our momentum slowed to a snail's pace as we painfully proceeded through tentacles of tree branches, stabbing and grabbing us. By the time we made it to the top, we had scraped up our faces, shoulders, and stomachs pretty good, and we couldn't wait to get out of there and never climb it again. It was no wonder that only one person recorded an ascent of Potash Knob on Peakbagger before this: some guy named Arthur Josephson from New Hampshire who referred to himself as "The PeakMaster." At the time, Arthur ranked third on Peakbagger for most recorded mountain ascents EVER. I'd like to know how "The PeakMaster" felt about being in third place.

There were a couple of other guys I kept track of on Peakbagger as well. Greg Slayden, the guy who started the site, climbed far fewer peaks than Arthur, but went after more challenging mountains with more vertical gain. Then there's Dave Dunham, a mountain runner from Massachusetts who held some records in the Mount Washington road race and seemed to be bunny-hopping his way around New England on a daily basis, straining for the fastest time on every mountain he climbed. Some of his entries looked as though he was in a race against time; like he could outpace Death itself if he could only move fast enough. Who were these guys? Were they like me, searching for answers? Or were they just trying to get away from it all?

Maybe the common thread was what Slayden said on his bio page, in that the main purpose of all this climbing is "existential." Climbing the 4000-footers, or climbing any mountain, opens you up to rewards and failure, which leads to self-discovery. Self-discovery allows you explore parts of yourself that you haven't before. To try things you haven't tried before. But perhaps mostly, climbing brings to focus the connection of hand to rock, foot to earth, and that you are but one person in a large, connected world. That while you may have headed up the mountain to get away from it all, the climb reminds you that you are perpetually, wonderfully, tied to those waiting for you back home, and your existence means something to more than you alone.

Chapter 29

Over the Hill

The well-trod Zealand Trail ran a little differently than most of the other trails I encountered in the Whites. Open and flat beginnings led to a beautiful panorama of the lower valley, before crossing the marshy Zealand Pond on one of the lengthiest foot bridges you can find. I suspected the AMC hut crews had a hand in its pristine condition. The extra care given to the entire trail was noticeable, a credit to them and I'm sure a host of volunteer trail-workers. If only there was something they could do about the smell. Where the oaks and maple play at the lower elevations, an odiferous funk swelled up from the piles of fallen leaves, soaked with rain and dew. Woooeee, it was RIPE. The omnipresent waft of decay made me wonder if a bear could even smell me coming. Food for thought.

A twenty-mile hike up Zealand and the three mountains commonly referred to as "The Bonds"—West Bond, Bond and Bondcliff—were on the day's itinerary. I was also going to slip in Mount Guyot, which wasn't on the AMC 4000-footer list, but was on Greg Slayden's Peakbagger.com list of NH's 4000-footers, replacing South Hancock from the AMC list. Greg explained the need for the second list as follows: "The AMC list does not include Mount Guyot, which appears to have the necessary 160 feet of clean prominence (200 feet optimistic). But it does include South Hancock, with 159 feet (199 optimistic) of prominence." I didn't exactly know what that meant except that now I would have to complete the AMC list *and* Greg's stupid list to cover all my bases. Thanks a lot Greg. You see how sick this all is?

It would be nice if after climbing so many mountains, it got easier to knock off some more, but the day was a mental struggle. I didn't want to climb when I woke that morning, and that feeling followed me up the trail. My body was stiff and sore, and I had to dig deep to find that little grit within that tells you to try harder and do what you didn't think you could do. To help, I thought about Prefontaine and how he liked to say that the reason he won so many races was because he was capable of taking on more pain than his competitors. Channeling his mindset, I shut off the part of my brain that was telling me to stop and go home.

When I reached the summit of West Bond, the winds were whipping all around me. Under the circumstances, it hardly felt like a place where one would linger and yet, wedged between the rocks beneath my feet were a couple of fresh cigarette butts, mixed in with some candy bar wrappers and a plastic bottle. *Who does that?* It had taken eight miles and several hours to get here, as the route crossed over the summits of Zealand and Guyot. How could someone litter here and want to breathe in all of this nature with a couple of death sticks? *Dude, look at this amazing, beautiful, isolated wilderness—let's rip some butts!*

What really got me was the trash though. It was one thing to see trash at the start of the Zealand Trail, where casual hikers carelessly dropped cigarette packs, beer cans, and food wrappers. There was nothing startling about that. Indeed, my expectations of humanity drop in accordance with earth's elevations. But up here? On the summit, eight miles in? You're going to leave trash? The people who made it this far into the wilderness are supposed to be my fellow Prefontaines. They're supposed to be better. I mean, who can I count on for a little help if not them? Am I all alone here?! *Geesh, I guess I'm turning into quite a crunchy.*

I'm kind of obsessed with trash. Not only for what it does to our sacred earth, but for what it does to our lives. Consider this: try holding a piece of trash in your hand for an hour. Feel the weight of it pulling on you, even if it's something light, like a wrapper. Try walking around with it, going to work with it, going out to dinner with it. Would drive you crazy, right? Instinctively you'd want to put it down the moment it arrived in your hand. If it can drive you crazy to hold a piece of trash for an hour, or even a minute, imagine what all the other junk you own is doing to you?

As forty approaches, you become increasingly aware of the fact that much of the first half of your life was spent obtaining things. You work, you buy a house, and then you fill that house with a bunch of stuff that will give you and your family a comfortable life. You are in acquisition mode, building a launch pad for your descendants to vault off of. You show your kids the ropes, you forge friendships, and you climb the mountain of life. (Okay, you knew I had to do it, didn't you? One cannot talk about turning forty and climbing mountains without noting the proverbial "getting over the hill.")

By the time you hit forty, maybe your oldest kids are around ten years old or thereabouts, and if things have gone well enough, you have most of what you need. *Except their college tuition money.* Now it's time to start throwing out some of the crap you've collected over the years: their old toys, the multiple blenders you got from your wedding, the junk filling up the back of the closet you haven't opened in a decade. As you whittle your own stuff down, you notice your kids' pile of crap growing. They are on their way up the hill, and to help simplify their lives, you throw some of their crap out too (when they're not looking). Middle age, I've come to learn, is largely centered around refuse management, and I'm frequently terrified by the thought that age forty to eighty will be an endless trip to the dump until I reach that point where I'm sending family members the last of my treasured keepsakes, piecemeal. Just forty years of throwing stuff out until you end up with very little; a return to where you started. *Alright, Matt, let's lighten up.*

But that's only if you focus on crap. If my house burnt down to the ground today, I could move on with little problem. Stuff is just stuff. You can't take it with you wherever you go, and you certainly can't take it with you when you're dead. As I move forward with the next forty years of my life, I don't want it to be about what I have, but about people and adventure. I don't want forty to be the top of the hill—I want it to be the base of it. I want to experience times and places I haven't seen before, and never stop looking for inspiration. Inspiration is something you can carry with you forever, and never weighs you down. But possessions?

Looking up from the trash on West Bond, I tried to triangulate my position, not knowing how to actually do that. West Bond had no discernable summit marker, and I wanted to make sure I was in the right place before attempting Mount Bond (proper). I looked over my phone map, guessed where I was relative to the other peaks I could identify, and figuring correctly, made my way to Mount Bond. At the summit I bumped into four French Canadians, all of whom had the tiniest little heads and were wearing ridiculously big smiles. They also looked considerably wet even though they weren't sweating, as if they brought hair styling gel for the journey. During pleasantries I gave the air a little sniff to see if these were the miscreants who left trash at the top of West Bond, but I didn't smell a trace of cigarette smoke on them.

Over the course of the day, I kept bumping into a guy in his fifties who said he had climbed all of the 4000-footers before and was working on his grid. We bumped into each other again on Bond, where he told me that he was going to leave Bondcliff for another day. Before leaving, he warned me that if I did continue on, it can be difficult returning over the rough terrain from Bondcliff at the end of a long day. But there was no going back for me. I was nine miles into the climb, with only 1.2 miles left to reach Bondcliff. I didn't come all this way to go back now.

The trail leading down from Mt. Bond to Bondcliff is craggy and angular, making it easy to twist your ankle. But it's also very exposed, and after a few thousand feet, I saw this eighteen-year-old kid appear, moving fast, looking to overtake me before I made it to my final summit. *Not today, kid.* With wobbly legs, I charged the last half mile while the speedy youth closed the gap. Every time I looked over my shoulder, he was twenty feet closer. *How are you doing that?* I was desperate to keep him at bay. Thankfully, when he was within five hundred feet of me, I made summit.

I had been hoping to finish my forty-eight on the iconic Bondcliff, where hikers stand on a rock pulpit overlooking the valley below—a sheer cliff dropping a thousand feet. Even though I still had to go back and climb Isolation to make it official, Bondcliff was the beginning of the end for me, and I was elated that I had arrived at this point. A lady who said she was from Henniker arrived at the summit wearing a leg brace and informed me that Bondcliff was number forty-eight for her—she was finished. We took pictures of each other and offered congratulations after I gave a qualified explanation of my mishap on Isolation. In my heart I knew what I accomplished, but if anyone were to ask me, I wasn't yet going to be able to look anyone in the eye and say, "Yes, I did them all."

It took over twenty miles to complete Zealand, the Bonds, and Guyot, and everything went according to plan. *Finally*. Almost at the end of my journey, my route planning, pack preparations, and understanding of my limits and the terrain were all spot on. Now, when I researched a route, I could accurately judge how long it would take and how to alter plans based on unexpected events. I felt like an expert.

When I got home that night, Liz and my youngest two, Jake and Phoebe, congratulated me at the door with hugs, kisses, and carrot cake—my favorite. They totally surprised me because in my mind I technically wasn't finished. Jake and Phoebe asked me all sorts of questions: Was it hard? Do you hurt? How long was it? Are you sore?

Excited that the kids were interested in what I'd been up to, I debriefed them in great detail, letting them know exactly how hard it was. They were, after all, the ones I was doing it for in an odd way. To perhaps inspire them a little and give them a story about their dad to reflect upon. I'd been giving a lot of thought lately about how parents need to be better at telling their story to their kids, no matter their age, before they die. Too often the stories of our ancestors get lost. You might remember some of it now, bits of it later, but eventually it wanes and then it goes. How nice would it be for your kids to be able to tell their grandkids why you did the things you did and the kind of person you were? *As long as you're not a jerk!*

I also hoped that my efforts in the woods would give all of my kids something to consider, outside the sensational buzz of game apps and social media. At the moment I was particularly worried for my oldest two, Chloe and Max, who were rapidly approaching their teenage years. I wondered how they would navigate the years to come and pave the way for their siblings. Kid life seems so much more complicated nowadays than it did in the nineties, when we all grew up in a bubble of safety, free of school shooters, terrorism, smartphones, and the internet.

During our carrot cake celebration, Max was deeply invested in a game of Words With Friends, where he routinely beat his former teacher and several of his great-aunts. I knew Max thought the climbing was awesome, but in the moment, he had the world of linguistic domination to attend to. He took a quick break to congratulate me with a warm, proud smile, and then returned to the task of dropping fifty-point words on Aunt Ellen. Little did he know that I was already plotting to get him out climbing with me.

Chloe was upstairs in her room during the festivities, so afterwards I went up to say goodnight to her. I stood in her doorframe for a moment and watched her work at her desk on yet another extra credit assignment she had given herself. Only in third grade, she was incredibly bored with the amount of work her teachers gave her, so she elected to do more, which I'm sure her teachers were all too happy to occupy her with. Eventually she noticed my presence and said, "Oh yay Dad, you're home from your big climb, and you are done with all of your mountains, although you really still have one mountain left because you technically didn't do it. Yayyyy. Congrats." Then she turned back towards her work. Chuckling to myself, I went to bed and crashed. I wasn't the only one trying to keep me honest.

The next day I woke, stiff as a board. Rigor mortis stiff. Like, wow stiff. Nothing felt quite right. Even my heart felt a little sluggish or slow or something. *It was probably good I did all of these before turning forty . . .*

Chapter 30

The Last Twenty Feet

After failing to climb Isolation, Liz, my parents, and everyone I knew said that it was okay I was only twenty feet shy of the summit; I could claim the mountain officially climbed. Nobody would have to know the truth. But in my heart, I knew it was false and I couldn't let it go. I'm critical of Bryson simply for putting a bear on the cover of his book; how could I claim I did the whole forty-eight if I had twenty feet left undone?

If I'm being honest, I'm a little too hard on Bryson. His book *A Walk in the Woods* is, in fact, a great book, and despite the false intrigue created by the bear on the cover, Bryson's claim that he did the Appalachian trail rings true, even though he never actually completed it. Because the point of the Appalachian trail is the same as the 4000-list: not to give you a list to conquer, but to offer you a framework to slow down, be present, and experience the wonders of the natural world. To invite you to connect with nature and reconnect with yourself as a result. But when it comes to honesty, I think you should take it pretty seriously. The world is full of fallacies and falsehoods perpetuated by other people: memoirs that didn't happen, résumés that are faked, rumors that aren't true. I want better, don't you? In my mind, nothing I say would be worth a minute of your time unless I went back to climb those last twenty feet.

It was the first of November, and I was regretting having missed my chance to summit the last time I went up the Glen Boulder Trail. It was hard enough in the summertime, when the ground was clear, but today there was already a surprising amount of snow clogging up the trail. Even with snowshoes on, my feet kept plunging deep into the postholes made by previous hikers. It was slow going, sinking down a couple of feet, hoisting my legs back onto another snowdrift, and then sinking down again.

Over the long slog, my thoughts drifted to places I'd rather be, like the day before. Halloween was hilarious. My dad was in charge of candy distribution, and he ran a tight ship. He had to because we get over two thousand kids that come to our house—no, really, we've counted. You've never seen anything like it. The town donates two thousand pieces of candy to us every year and we still have to buy three thousand more to ensure we can give out two pieces per kid. The system usually works out pretty well.

But on this Halloween, some mothers sent their kids up to the candy table without a bag, in order to limit their candy acquisition to one measly piece. My dad, a candy connoisseur of the highest order, took offense, and decided to enforce these mothers' rules out of spite. So when a bagless kid reached in for more than one piece, Dad grabbed the kid's hand and yelled, "No! You only get one! Your mom said you couldn't!" In a culture where nobody is allowed to touch or chastise another person's kid anymore, kids were stricken pale by the dozen. Right after admonishing the bagless, he then rewarded the kids carrying bags with handfuls of candy. Everyone was confused about this new world order, but as children fled from the sixty-six-year-old man muttering about people ruining Halloween, you better believe there was dissention in the ranks when the bagless kids returned to their mothers.

I let out a laugh thinking about it. How great is it that we have holidays like Halloween to give us a set date to enjoy our family with? That no matter how fast life moves, we have these intermittent pitstops baked into the calendar, forcing us to come together and experience our families and all the color they provide. I know family holidays are often something people dread and can sometimes feel like a giant "have-to," but the purpose they serve is fantastic when you really think about it. Like a big climb, they force you to decelerate, pause, and fully appreciate the people that care about you most, while maybe giving you a chance to reexamine yourself a bit as well.

I kept thinking about my family the entire hike up Isolation. What I want for them. What I don't. How they told me it didn't matter if I did this. How it mattered to me that they knew that I did. In the thick snowpack, I think I was averaging a mile per hour, but it didn't bother me how long it was taking. I had plenty to reflect on. When I finally got to the spot that I *believed* was the summit two months before, I found the spur trail leading to the top in a few short seconds. It was so obvious, I wanted to punch myself. *It's right there, how did I miss it?* Five minutes later I was standing at the summit and had to laugh at myself: I endured six miles of a painful, sopping wet climb over rock and snow, all for another twenty vertical feet that nobody cared if I did or not. I may have learned a lot through this adventure, but I was still an idiot.

Standing there, mission completed, I didn't feel anything euphoric like I did on many of my other climbs. I didn't feel inspired to return to this spot again, or think of where my climbing would take me next. I paused to reflect, not out of instinct, but because I felt like I was supposed to. There was no grand epiphany here, no sudden wisdom revealed. Only the recurring thought that I was glad that I had stayed true to myself and did what I had set out to do. I could look myself in the eye.

It was 4:15 and getting pretty late to still be out on Isolation, especially because I hadn't seen a soul all day. I was, well, isolated. It was time to get back to the real world. But as I made my way towards the Rocky Branch, I considered that this wasn't the end of my climbing adventures at all. With these mountains not merely under my belt, but in my being, I envisioned many more mountain adventures to come. Maybe not an all-out blitz campaign like this again, but definitely more to come, especially with my kids.

After promising myself I'd never take the Rocky Branch trail again, I learned from my Instagram hiking community that it wasn't too bad in the wintertime, and they were right. The snow was still a foot deep in most places, which slowed my pace more than I expected, but I didn't have to contend with all the roots and mud from my summer adventure, and the trail was soft on my feet. Night fell at 6pm, and I descended the last hour and a half in the dark. When I arrived at Pinkham Notch Road, I was two hours behind schedule, but I didn't mind.

The final leg of my journey was a three-and-a-half-mile trek down Route 16 to my car at the Glen Ellis parking lot. Along the way, there were four monster hills to climb, and as I started out it began to rain a little. Not much—barely enough to warrant putting on my rain jacket, but I put it on anyway. It was cold out, but the rain didn't creep into my spine as it normally would under such conditions. Instead, I felt oddly comfortable, as if enveloped in a warm, ethereal hug. Years and years ago, I used to think that rain might be God, or Mary, crying up in heaven, and I kidded myself that one of them was sad that my journey was coming to an end.

The temperature started dropping and the rain turned into little flecks of snow. How fitting, I thought, that snow should accompany me at both the start and end of my journey. Walking along the highway's edge, the air ever so silent from the falling snow, I supposed I should have been lonely. But I had come a long way from the rube fumbling around on Moosilauke, running from a blizzard I was unprepared to meet. The approaching headlights of a few cars were the only other pairs of eyes I'd seen that day, and on other days, exhausted and worn out, I would have tried to flag them down. But today I was quite content to leg it out in the freezing cold, the frosty snow kissing my face, and embrace the lonely steps. I wasn't alone at all. I had me.

I've often heard that people feel a big letdown after achieving a significant goal or summit, or completing some major challenge that was before them. That after accomplishing something of importance, they feel empty the next day because their purpose is now gone, and they need something new to tackle. It's why after climbing the 4000-footers of New Hampshire you can keep going and climb all of the 4000-footers in New England. But I didn't feel empty on the walk to my car or in the days that followed. All I felt was satisfaction in knowing that I did something that I had been wanting to do for more than twenty years.

The 4000-footer list could include twenty mountains or one hundred, it's all the same. The list is nothing more than a prescription to help us get out there and find ourselves again. To remember the earth again, sense it, and tap into the restorative power it provides. It doesn't matter if you climb all of the mountains on the list, one of them, or choose to avoid mountains altogether and keep your outdoor excursions limited to the flatlands. The list doesn't matter at all. All that matters is the going.

Chapter 31

What a Nutjob

The next day I did what any respectable hard-core mountaineer would do and shared my successful completion of the 4000-footers on Instagram. This prompted a congratulatory call from my dad, who said, "I loved your post. Do you want to hear what your mother said after I read her the part about you walking along the highway? Well, she put down her book, looked at me, and said, 'What a nutjob!' Isn't that hysterical?" He started guffawing and between laughs managed to say, "About her own son! A nutjob!" I loved it and laughed along with him.

To mark the accomplishment, my awesome wife surprised me with some commemorative T-shirts for me and the whole family. On the front read "#nh48" and on the back were all of the hashtags I had used when I posted pictures of my climbs. An incredible token to remind me of how far I'd come, not only with my climbing, but my social media savvy as well. Okay fine, maybe not savvy, but certainly a willingness to share who I am and what I'm about. Before this adventure, I always thought I was an open book, but I learned along the way that there were significant parts of me I was still holding back. This experience not only helped me get over the fact I was turning forty; it initiated a reexamination of the person I want to be, prompting me to make steps in that direction.

With the mountains now behind me, there was only one thing left to do to round out this whole experience: apply to become an official member of the "AMC Four Thousand Footer Club." The requirements for application involved submitting a successful ascent list of the forty-eight, the dates each mountain was climbed, and a brief description of how each journey went. You also had to submit a short essay regarding the last peak on the list you summited, along with a $10 application fee, naturally. I sent them a riveting account of my pains on Isolation and a check for $100. They certainly deserved it, and I hoped the extra $90 would find its way towards future trail work on the Rocky Branch.

The 60th Annual Meeting and Awards Night was held on April 22, 2017, at Exeter High School. In the audience that night there were reportedly six hundred people, and nine hundred people receiving awards altogether. The event wasn't only for people completing the New Hampshire Forty-Eight either. Awards were also given to those who completed the New England Sixty-Seven 4000-

footers, the hundred highest peaks in New England, the New Hampshire forty-eight exclusively in the wintertime, and the Northeast 111 Club, reserved for the truly dedicated who have climbed all of the 4000-footers in the northeastern United States. *Hmmm. More dreams to ponder.*

Before the awards were handed out, Liz and I took the kids over to enter a few of the raffles put on by EMS, meet some of my fellow climbers over dinner, and answer some trivia questions while perusing the books and photographs presented by the club. Everywhere you looked were smiling faces, and it was clear that everyone was feeling quite proud of themselves for their accomplishments.

At dinner, I met a man who recently completed redlining a large swath of New England. It was a little unclear to me how much climbing he was talking about, but I think he meant that he had hiked every trail in New England that can be found on any of the AMC maps, of which there are hundreds. He was so proud of the fact that there were less than a hundred people in the world who are known to have done that, he was beside himself. My family's matching #nh48 T-shirts didn't seem so extreme anymore.

By the time we made it into the auditorium for the award ceremony, I couldn't help but notice that most of the people there were in their sixties or twenties. Clearly, this was a hobby for those with free time: retirees and failure-to-launch millennials. There were a few families sprinkled into the mix, but few midlife crisis sufferers that I could discern. The other forty-year-olds I met on the trails must have been taking a more sensible, protracted approach, to embracing these mountains.

After a few introductory remarks, a twenty-minute music video was played, featuring pictures and quotes submitted by some of the climbers receiving certificates. The images told the story of all people, young and old, pushing themselves to experience the euphoria of climbing a big mountain. Some photos showed climbers raising their arms in exaltation, while others captured moments of exhaustion, tears, and heartfelt embraces. There were scenes of hikers watching sunsets, wading through rivers, and gazing out at the valley from another glorious summit success. One shot even showed a woman with a gray jay perched on her head.

Some climbers held up signs with the numbers 48, 67, 100, or 111, marking their milestones, while others held up pictures of loved ones who had passed—husbands, wives, mothers, and fathers, carried with them while they processed their grief. There were summit toasts, celebrations with dogs and friends, and a couple of mountaintop proposals. Some faces were actually familiar—people I had seen out on the trail or followed on Instagram. As I watched the faces go by on the screen, I realized that they all shared a profound look of redemption, and that when I was out there alone on the trails, I was never alone at all. Their stories were my story, and mine was theirs. Age and circumstance were irrelevant.

At one point during the video they posted a quote that read, "Hiking is generally a great opportunity to get away from society, materialism, advertisements, expectations, and stupidity." *Ah yeah, that pretty much sums it up.* Now comfortably secure that we were among likeminded people, the audience joined in a singalong of "I Climbed Every Mountain," which was specifically about climbing the 4000-footers. It gave everyone a good laugh to try and keep up with the chorus: "Well I've been down every trail, and I never took the Cog Rail, I climbed, I climbed every mountain . . . Isolation, Waumbek, Whiteface, Galehead, Jackson, Tom, Bondcliff, Cannon . . ." Everyone got messed up with the flow from Jackson to Tom, and the rhythm was never fully recovered after that.

When the singalong was over, the club leaders got down to the business of calling off names, which went on for a couple of hours. After more than eight hundred names were called, we were beginning to wonder if they forgot me. I have an odd, long, unlucky history of being the forgotten man on lists, or drawing the short straw, or picking the worst option out of a hat, and it wouldn't have surprised me at all if my name wasn't called. But when they surpassed nine hundred names, it was getting really worrisome that we made our four-year-old daughter suffer through this whole thing for no reason at all. She was rolling her eyes and pulling on her cheeks, rapidly losing her mind. We needed mercy. When the speaker said, "and the last certificate to be given out tonight goes to" . . . Liz and I looked at each other and couldn't stop laughing until I was back in my seat with my certificate.

Two minutes after naming me the last recipient of the evening, my oldest daughter won first pick in the EMS raffle. When she headed up to the stage to make her selection, the EMS rep spoke with a low voice into the microphone: "Take the tent kid. Make your parents happy." Considering the rest of the gear from EMS was mainly shirts and hats, it was a total score. Lucky. As I watched her and my family celebrate the win, I kept thinking I was the luckiest guy in the room.

Chapter 32

The Hardest Mountain

I used to think I was pretty tough because I had climbed some big mountains and gone on some pretty wild adventures. I took on Grand Teton in a rainstorm that never let up. I conquered Kilimanjaro with altitude sickness that had me retching and unable to stomach food for three days. Harder than that was Mount Rainier—a hellish four-day trudge up glacial snow, carrying a fifty-pound pack. On each one of those climbs, reports came in that another climber had died on the trail up ahead of us, but I had lived, and with that came the false sense that I, and my friends, were a little stronger and a little smarter than some other climbers. That I was more prepared to handle whatever life threw at me. Then came the night of October 8th, 2017.

For reasons still unclear to the medical community, I awoke in the middle of the night with petechiae, stabbing pains in both shoulders, and insane nausea. My body was ice-cold, and I was having trouble seeing. I couldn't take a step without the room spinning, and the pinky and ring fingers in both hands were twitching uncontrollably. I was pretty sure I was dying, but to make extra sure, I waited two hours to see if it would pass. It didn't, so I woke Liz up to take me to the emergency room at 3am.

At the ER they found a blocked kidney, but didn't think that was the problem, so they gave me some meds to calm my system, ran a bunch of tests, and then cleared me to leave without any explanation for what happened. Six days later, I was back in the ER again, this time because pins and needles developed throughout my entire body, but most alarmingly in my head. They thought I was having a stroke, but all CAT scans came back normal. Then they thought I had pancreatitis, but I hadn't been drinking. Whatever was happening, my entire nervous system was going completely haywire. After going on a precautionary liquid diet, I slowly introduced food, but it couldn't be done without incredible pain, nausea, or the pins and needles coursing their way through my body. Even water caused debilitating spasms. Ever since that week, I haven't had a single day without electric jolts running through my spine or burning pain in the soft muscle tissue surrounding my esophagus, kidney and lower back.

Over the last several years I've seen a whole host of "specialists" from some of the best hospitals in New England, many of whom didn't think my symptoms were real, but a manifestation of some mental health issue. The allergist I saw thought I was crazy, it's all in my head. The neurologist I saw thought I was crazy but would love to do some experiments involving electricity. *No thanks! I'm already getting electrocuted!* A nurse suggested I was having anxiety and all that I needed was a good book to read, but I'm not an anxious guy. Well, I wasn't until all of these medical professionals wouldn't listen to me. But when this all started, I had no thoughts of cancer or dying, and going to the doctor was the last thing on my mind. I had gone for a four-mile run the day before my first trip to the ER and hadn't even lost my breath. *I was going to live forever!* A few months earlier I was standing on the summit of Mount Isolation and felt like I was in the prime of my life.

Every doc I went to listened to my story, said "weird," and then suggested I see someone else, and probably a psychiatrist. Wondering if this really was all some sort of weird panic attack, I started meditating. The mantra "I am a river" popped into my head, and I repeated it over and over again to get myself through each day, hoping the pain would pass through me and leave me be. With no medical help to turn to, I found myself praying to God to please give me another ten years so that I could get my kids to adulthood.

The tingling in my head felt like something was eating my brain. I couldn't sleep for more than an hour at a time, and often woke to find my body shivering. The worst was every time I ate, these stabbing pains would hit me in the shoulders like someone was sticking me with a knife. Some nights the pain was so bad it brought me to tears, but I couldn't take anything for the pain because that would increase the pins and needles in my head again. It felt like I was caught in the world's worst catch-22. Night after night I watched hours of bad movies on Netflix, while researching the internet for answers.

While waiting for kidney surgery, there were some really scary nights where my body wouldn't stop shaking and I thought I was going to die. A gastroenterologist thought the issue was in my gut and recommended probiotics, which shockingly led to an abnormally slow heartbeat and, of all things, a bloody tongue. I was scared. When the first ER doc told me about the "large, cystic structure inside my kidney," forty years of life plans flew before my eyes and time stopped. I was reminded of how tenuous life is. As my father used to say, this whole thing we call life is a "crapshoot." It's not fair, it's not uniform, and it's not to be taken lightly. But what was happening to me was more than a kidney problem: my body was rejecting every kind of medicine being thrown at it. Watching blood trickle off my tongue in the mirror late at night, my heart laboring to give me the energy to even walk, I believed the end was near. And in those moments when you are scared about losing your life, you dwell on what you would do if you had another year of health. Another week of it. Another day.

When I was climbing and in all the years before it, I felt a great deal of responsibility to be the best man I could be for everyone around me. But now I didn't feel the need to be the man anymore. All I wanted now was to spend time with my family and friends, love them, and share experiences with them. It no longer mattered to me if I was strong enough to take care of all of them; it would be enough to simply be with them and enjoy them. Life was no longer about how much I've done, or how many mountains I've climbed, but how much time can I get with my family. Can I get more time? Can I get more quality time? Will I ever have a day without pain again? Forget climbing mountains, it would be enough if I only got to look upon them again.

For the last two thousand five hundred and thirty-one days—almost seven years—I've been inching my way up the hardest mountain I've ever climbed, one foot in front of the other. After getting surgery for my kidney, the pins and needles and the sharp shoulder pains immediately went away. *So much for that not causing any of my problems.* It took a lot longer though to figure out why I kept getting electrocuted whenever I ate or exercised, or even when I went to the bathroom. Finally, a year later I found a doc who determined that I had extensive nerve damage as a result of something called Mast Cell Activation Syndrome. Even with a diagnosis, the medication they gave me only caused more damage, leaving me no choice but to push forward each day, medication-free. Relying on exercise, nutrition, meditation, and a few other tricks like grounding to cope with the agonizing nerve regeneration, I continue to hold onto the hope that this nightmare will someday stop. Happily, I can say that I'm getting closer and closer to being the man I was before my first ER visit, but of course, even if I fully heal, I'll never truly be that guy again.

We are all dealt adversity in life that we've got to deal with, and while we may not be at fault for it, we all have to take responsibility for it. For too long I kept putting all of my hope into doctors to tell me what was wrong, and to fix it, and they had nothing for me. Scores of "the best" doctors money can buy, and they had nothing. It took me a while before I realized that Larry Bird wasn't coming through that door. Nobody was coming to help. That for me, there was no normal answer to solve the riddle of my pain, because everything that the doctors gave me made the pain worse. All I could do was take each day as it comes, face the pain rather than run from it, and look at things through the brightest lens possible. And eventually, when I did all that, things did start to get better. Slowly, but they did.

I'm not all the way back, but can *feel* it coming back, and that's enough for me to feel very grateful. Maybe I'll have a day without pain again, and maybe I won't. But I'm alive, and that is plenty to celebrate. It took me a little while but ultimately, I realized that no matter how bad I felt, I had so much to be thankful for: a great wife, great kids, a great job, expensive health insurance that could help me afford all these shitty doctors who couldn't help. Focusing on such positives helped me to stop dwelling on the lost time I was experiencing and get back to living. The key was to finally face the mountain, as scary as it often looked, appreciate that I am still here to see it, and start climbing again.

Epilogue

A Letter to My Kids

I know I've always told you that I plan to live to a hundred and twenty. I still do, but in truth, I always had a feeling that I was only slated for forty years in this world. As far back as I can remember, I've felt terrible. Like there was a fog in my head and something was eating at my body. Asthma, chronic allergies, never-ending sinus infections, lifelong arthritis, and a constant ebb and flow of medical mishaps gave me a sense of impending doom I couldn't shake. I used to think that if I made it to forty-one, it would be a great victory over the opposing will of nature; over the will of God. During these last, almost seven years of chronic pain, I often questioned why God was treating me so, but now I feel that I've received a tremendous gift. I can't imagine taking another day for granted again. Ever.

When I was growing up some of my friends used to call me Lucky Larson because they said good things, amazing things, always seemed to happen to me. According to them, I always seemed to go out with the girl I liked, or go wherever I wanted, or do anything I wanted. I had tons of friends and lots of people I loved. And they were right. I was blessed with good fortune, but there was a reason. What my friends didn't see was the bad luck. The countless nights struggling to breathe. The constant hammering in my knees. The time I got mono in my liver and missed my only chance to sail in the U.S. Nationals. The broken back and subsequent years of pain. Shingles when I was twenty-five. C-diff when I was thirty-three. All the lost time from health issues that led me to make moves a little faster and with a bit more gusto when I was healthy enough. It was the bad luck that made me Lucky Larson.

Did I envy other's good health growing up? Sure did. Do I now? Nope. Every little struggle I've experienced has given me such great appreciation for how quickly this could all be over, and I know that I could have it much, much worse. So why stew in what's been lost when there is so much to gain? You can look at life with a half glass empty view, lamenting your poor fortune, or you can say, "You know what? I've got something in front of me that I have to conquer and dammit, I am going to do it, because today is another day and it's a good day to be alive." Every day is an opportunity, regardless of our condition, for new experiences and new connections. For adventure and inspiration. Catching a small glimpse of the sand filtering out of the hourglass has led me to live the best life I can, no matter how bad I'm feeling, and make my own luck.

When I was sixteen, I knew I wanted a wife and four kids—exactly two boys and two girls, if God would be so kind. I got lucky and got exactly what I wanted, but setting my mind towards it certainly helped turn that vision into a reality. Obviously, life throws you all sorts of curveballs, and not everything will work out the way you like, but if you never make a plan for your vision, it's more likely to never happen. Not everything has to be planned, but for the big stuff, you will come much closer to achieving some semblance of your dreams if you make a plan for them and visualize them, rather than hoping fate will drop them into your lap.

When you do set your vision for how you want your life to look, and who with, don't just make a plan and then wait for something to happen later. Apply for that job *now*. Study hard *now*. Call that girl *now*. Plan your next adventure *now*. Stop thinking about it and go for it. And don't let others wreck your vision. Don't be deterred by those who tell you no, you can't. Or that you're going to fail. Who cares if you fail? You'll never know what you're capable of if you don't try, and life is shaped by both the risks we did and didn't take. None of you would be here if your mom didn't marry me, and she never would have married me if I didn't take the chance of moving back home to Boston to see if I could find her and get her to go on a date with me. *How do you like them apples, Matt Damon?*

There are all sorts of different things you can do with this life, and it's usually the odd ones that end up having the stories worth telling. Don't worry what others think about your aspirations. Know that every person you know, except the critical few like your family, will probably disappear from your life eventually. People move on with their lives and one day you will wake up to find that it's been thirty years since you've seen someone you see every day right now. There is only one person you are guaranteed to see your whole life, and that's you!

So ask yourself, what do you want to do? What do you want to do today, tomorrow, next year, and with your life? The answers don't have to be big, or perfect, or "the one" that's going to help you figure out your whole life. There is no one idea, silver bullet, or magic arrow for that. Whatever dream you have, big or small, make a plan and take sensible steps. People may judge you and criticize you along the way. Some might even think you are weird. Hey, your mom thinks I'm weird sometimes, and that's okay, I probably am. But as long as she doesn't think "this weirdo is annoying," everything is right as rain.

To simplify things and keep your life moving in the right direction, the question you should frequently ask yourself is: What am I doing with my life right now? Not "What will I do with my life?" but "What am I doing with my life right *now?*" What can I do today that will make it more meaningful? It's important to set goals for the future, but don't waste time worrying about them. Focus on today and stay in the moment. And don't forget to root for yourself along the way.

I know we can harp on you about being kind to others, and how important it is to raise others up and champion their efforts, but you can't forget to root for yourself as well. You should root for yourself above all others, because you are the only one who has complete control of you. If your life is going well, then you will be better able to lift up those around you. That doesn't mean you beat others down to get where you want to go, but you rise above everyone else to help lift them up. Set a higher mark for yourself and set yourself apart. Root for yourself to be kinder, smarter, stronger, and more capable than everyone you meet, so that people can count on you to be those things, and better themselves as a result of knowing you.

Start with the little things: look people in the eye when you say hello, shake their hand, greet them with warmth, be kind, give of yourself generously through every simple aspect of your life, whether you are at the desk, out in the field, out with friends, or wherever life takes you. Learn from the mistakes you made yesterday. Acknowledge them and then aim to be better today. That's all you need to do. You do that, and good things will happen. But be willing to make mistakes! Mistakes are good! Make them and own them. Mistakes make you great.

Mistakes are made by people who try. Like we always say when you are skiing: if you ain't falling, you ain't trying. So try. Fall. Repeat. Until you don't fall anymore. Then find something new to stumble over. Pick another mountain to climb. Sometimes you will get to the summit, sometimes you won't. *But keep climbing and living!* Keep learning and be mindful of your experiences. Reflect as you go. Whatever happens you will have a story to tell, and a shared story is one that kindles the light over and over again in the retelling. Don't be one of those people who can only tell you what happened on the latest episode of their favorite TV program. Everyone yearns for deeper meaning, and you can't find it by living your life on the sidelines, afraid of what people will think. You will never be able to make everyone happy and you shouldn't endeavor to do so.

Looking back, there have been so many embarrassing moments in my life. So many mistakes. That's just life. You'll have them too. Things that seem like a big deal now will be something you'll laugh about later. And you need to laugh about them because life should not be an awful thing to endure, but a wonderful thing to experience. Setbacks happen and you have to find a way to let them roll off your back and not define you. There are people that will help you along the way, and people who will bring you down, forget you, and cause interference. There will be times when the negative influences seem to outweigh the good ones, and they will fill your head with self-doubt. Forget them. Listen to those who say you can. And if you're the only one saying it, that's enough. Sometimes you will have nobody to draw faith from except that other person who lives inside your head. That bounce back persona that resides within, saying "You can do this." Trust that person.

You should know, my love for you is a gift that never has to be returned. All I want for you cannot be measured, and there is no cup big enough to fill what I hope for you. I want to see you live the best lives that you can and enjoy it as much as you can. I never want you to feel like you owe me anything because you think it's what I would want you to feel. I want you to act upon what you think is right, not upon what others want of you. I want you to be good, caring, generous, and loving people, and the only way I know how to lead you to that, is to love you unconditionally. That doesn't mean not holding you accountable for wrong actions or not being your parent when you break a window or crash the car. My relationship with you may have conditions. Our mutual respect for each other may have conditions. But my love for you does not. Everything I have done for you is not something I will ever hold over your heads. It is a gift, and there are no repayments required except giving yourself the best chance at being an excellent human being and treating others with the same respect you deserve. But you owe me nothing. It is I who owe you.

I owe it to you to show what a man should be. What a father and a husband should be. I owe it to you because of all that's been given to me, and the luck that's been bestowed upon me to have you. And someday, when you have children, everything you think you might owe me, you will pay to them. It's the ultimate form of paying it forward. And through your actions, I will earn my reward, because your success, and your children's success, is my success.

You do owe it to yourselves, however, to be big people. To give back to others what has been given to you. To always strive to surpass your current limitations as an individual and grow beyond them. Not out of a need for pride or self-congratulation, but out of an innate love and gratitude for the gift of life. You owe it to yourself to climb mountains that test your limits and let yourself know that you, and others, can rely on you when times get tough. Just promise your mother and me that whatever mountains you choose to climb, none of them will be in North Korea.

Climbing the forty-eight biggest mountains in New Hampshire is a small feat, and nothing compared to the many challenges of regular life: raising a family, providing for them, taking them to the hospital when they are sick, constantly worrying about them, making sure they turn into good men and women. Those are mountains. Those are HUGE mountains. Climbing the 4000-footers was a wonderful journey, but it can't hold a candle to the amazing adventure it has been raising you, and the sheer joy it is to be able to call myself your father.

On the road to becoming an adult, there will be many mountains to climb. Many conflicts to wrestle. You will have to figure things out on your own and fight to carve out a life for yourself that reflects your being. It doesn't matter if the challenges you face in life are things that could literally kill you or things that figuratively chip away at your soul. Whatever they are, the struggles are real, and rites of passage that every man and woman go through. Rich, poor, sick, healthy, nobody's life is easy street. Everyone has their battles to face, and that's what makes life interesting. Your job is to recognize life's challenges, rise to meet them, and then beat them back until you become who you are supposed to be. Some mountains you may decide to tackle alone, as you should. You'll be better for it. But know that you never have to go it alone either. And if you ever want or need someone to go climbing with, say the word and I'm there.

Acknowledgements

First and foremost, I want to thank my wife, Liz, for her endless patience and support. I've learned so much during this journey and have become a better writer—and a better person—largely because of you.

To my father, Don, thank you for your unwavering belief in this project. You gave me the confidence to know I was on the right path. And to my mother, Mary, thank you for encouraging me to write when I was young. It helped lay the first brick from which a foundation was formed. I don't think I can ever fully express my gratitude to you both for all that you have done for me.

I'm also grateful to Margaret and Justin Nyweide, as well as Jonathan Ring, for their thoughtful insights and help in shaping this story into what it is today. Your voices came back to me throughout my revisions, and I'm so appreciative that you gave me the honest feedback I was looking for.

Similarly, I'd be remiss if I didn't share my appreciation for the endless words of encouragement from friends and family, convincing me that maybe my writing wasn't half bad. To the Kuppens and Larson clans in particular, thank you.

Many thanks also go to Danna Mathias Steele for bringing my vision to life with your beautiful cover design, and John Knight for your guidance during the editing process. Writing this book was an education, and you both made it considerably easier to navigate.

Finally, I'd like to thank my kids: Chloe, Max, Jake, and Phoebe. Your enthusiasm keeps my steps light and quick, ready for the next climb.

About the Author

Matt Larson started hiking in the White Mountains as a kid, over forty years ago, and immediately felt a deep connection to the region. Since that time, his fondness for the area has only grown. Always a writer at heart, his career distracted him for twenty-five years, limiting his opportunities to write. It only makes sense that the place where he first felt truly inspired during his childhood is what turned him back to his passion for writing.

Matt lives in New Hampshire with his wife, Liz, and their four children. When he's not writing, he's looking for ways to get them all out in the mountains together.

www.ingramcontent.com/pod-product-compliance
Lightning Source LLC
Chambersburg PA
CBHW060551080526
44585CB00013B/527